an Actor's Life

It's Better than Selling Shoes!

the life of
Bob Thompson

with Kerstin Conner

Beaver's Pond Press, Inc.
Edina, Minnesota

ISBN 1-59298-043-0

Library of Congress Catalog Number: 2003114008

Typesetting and design by Mori Studio

Printed in the United States of America

First Printing: November 2003

07 06 05 04 03   5 4 3 2 1

Beaver's Pond Press, Inc.

7104 Ohms Lane, Suite 216
Edina, MN 55439
(952) 829-8818
www.beaverspondpress.com

to order, visit *www.BookHouseFulfillment.com*
or call 1-800-901-3480. Reseller discounts available.

This book is dedicated to my dear wife, Margaret, and my family; to the memory of my parents and teachers who were steadfast in their faith that I might succeed, and to my many theatrical colleagues associated with numerous productions over the past 65 years, and finally to the appreciative audiences who responded so graciously to my efforts to entertain.

To all, thank you!

—Bob

Contents

Foreword

If first met the actor, Bob Thompson, when I contacted him about giving a program for the Ephraim Foundation about the history of the Peninsula Players in Fish Creek, Wisconsin. He agreed and in May 2002 he invited me to his Sister Bay home to discuss the presentation and help him select appropriate materials for it. When I arrived, he had what seemed to be *his whole life history spread out on the kitchen table*—playbills dating back fifty years, photographs, press clippings, videos—and my first thought was "my God, how is he going to fit all this into a one hour program at the Ephraim Moravian Church?" But my second thought was what a shame it would be if all this theatre history with Bob's vivid memories and amusing stories were to be lost; that they must be preserved not only for his family but also for those of us who are curious about the unique history of the Peninsula Players and Bob's life as an actor. His program at the church turned out to be a delightful reminiscence about his years at the Players and it concluded with a hilarious reading from Oscar Wilde's play, *The Importance of Being Earnest,* with Bob reprising his role as Lady Bracknell!

During one of our visits I had asked him if he had ever considered writing an autobiography because it was obvious that he had had a long and interesting life in the theatre. His response was he had already written forty pages during a Spanish holiday where, because of rain, he was cooped up in his hotel room for a week and was bored. I asked if I might read it and discovered it was both whimsical and sly with an understated humor which was most appealing! All it really needed was to be expanded into a full-length memoir.

The result was this book which has been almost a year long collaboration of tape recorded interviews and telephone conversations. Fortunately, Bob is a "saver" and his basement was filled with voluminous folders of letters, fascinating photographs, and press clippings—his entire theatrical career spanning almost sixty-five years was there to be examined and shaped into what has become his autobiography. In his lengthy career he had appeared with such stars as: Joe E. Brown, Mickey Rooney, Betty Grable, Howard Keel, June Havoc, Robert Wagner, Sandy Dennis, Kathy Crosby, Dina Merrill...the list just goes on and on! Over a thirty year period, he was one of Chicago's leading character actors having appeared in over 300 plays during his lifetime.

But his spiritual home has always been the Peninsula Players in Fish Creek, Wisconsin where he first appeared in 1938 while still a student at the Goodman Theatre School. This autobiography not only tells the story of his childhood, his Chicago acting career, and his forays on Broadway but also is a fascinating glimpse into the Peninsula Players history, its founder Caroline Fisher Rathbone, and those early actors who contributed so much to the theatre's tradition of excellence.

To write Bob's story was, for me, an act of faith. First of all, I was very conscious of the need to finish the manuscript as quickly as possible because he was 86 years old when we began this project and I wanted him to have the pleasure of seeing his life in print.

Our work together has been extremely gratifying for me, particularly because he and his wife, Margaret, are such warm and genuine people. When I think of Bob Thompson, the phrase which immediately comes to mind is, "a life, well lived!"

—Kerstin Conner

Acknowledgments

Iwould like to thank the following people who were interviewed and whose stories of either Bob Thompson or the Peninsula Players gave valuable insights to this book. Also included here are others who made equally important contributions to the project.

Todd Schmidt, Executive Producer, who gave his blessing to the endeavor and permission to use materials and photographs from Peninsula Players sources. Greg Vinkler, Artistic Director and actor; Playwright and actor, Tom Mula, who wrote *Bob Almighty*; Actress and director, Amy McKenzie; Bruce Mielke, Peninsula Players photographer since 1985 and his wife, Jan Mielke, who scanned and recopied all photographs used in this book; Maggy Magerstadt Rosner, retired actress whose witty reminiscences enlivened this story. James Maronek, scenic designer and Players apprentice 1950-53 for his stories of those early days. Special thanks to Héloise Rathbone for her candid portrait of the Fisher-Rathbone family. Richard Christiansen, retired theatre critic, *Chicago Tribune* for his thoughtful comments on Bob's career.

Thanks also to Margaret Thompson whose endless pots of coffee and sustaining lunches in her cozy kitchen helped keep up our strength during four weeks of interviews. Bob's sister, Eleanor Moyer of Petoskey, Michigan, for her story of Marion Foreman Rathbone and invaluable childhood photos from the family album. Thanks also to Bob's children for their interest in this project: David Thompson, Hollister, California; Kay Friedrich, Pensacola, Florida; and Don Thompson, Ellison Bay, Wisconsin.

Special thanks to my kind neighbor, Joan Redenius, a rifle-shot typist and computer genius who came to my rescue and typed the completed manuscript into Microsoft Word format.

Also to the following friends who provided food, comfort, and housing during out-of-town interviews: Tom and Gwen Brendel, Ephraim; Don and Marianne Recht, Chicago; and Shirley Loewe, New York City.

To my husband who gave his unquestioning encouragement and support to this endeavor – thank you, Dick!

Finally, and most importantly, to Bob Thompson himself for allowing me to tell his story.

Chapter 1
Garfield Park

I was born in Kansas City on October 7, 1916 and when I was two, I remember sitting on the front steps when a mysterious horse drawn wagon appeared in the street below. I caught just a glimpse of raven hair and gaudy clothing before my mother snatched me inside saying,

"Watch out, the gypsies will get you!!"

There was something magical about that wagon and as I listened to the tinkling bells slowly fading away into the distance, I remember thinking maybe I would like to go with them...

We must have moved to Chicago shortly thereafter because my next memories are of Garfield Park, which in the 1920's was an elegant and respectable neighborhood. We lived at 417 North Central Park Blvd. just one block from the Garfield Park Conservatory, a fragrant oasis of exotic flowers and palm trees in the midst of the noisy city. Streetcars ran near our block and I loved hearing the metallic clang of the conductor's bell, warning cars and pedestrians to get out of the way. Above Lake Street, the elevated train clattered along while beneath it was a steady stream of horse drawn vehicles, black sedans, and bicycles. A pervasive smell of chocolate from Bunte's Candy Factory lingered in the air. I was seven when I watched President Harding's funeral train slowly proceed along the Northwestern tracks with its whistles blowing and carriages draped with solemn black bunting.

My parents had married later in life. My mother, Grace Van Der Veer Thompson, was thirty-eight when I was born. She was a thoughtful, kindhearted woman who was born in 1878 in Raritan, a tiny farming community in western Illinois near the Mississippi River. How or where she met my father, Alfred A. Thompson, is a complete mystery to me. My parents never talked about their courtship, but I do know they were married in 1915 in Kansas City, Missouri where my father worked for General Electric. He was born in Berkeley, California in 1882, had graduated with a degree in electrical engineering from the University of California, and worked for GE all his life. It was the early days of hydro-electric power; he was a troubleshooter for the company traveling from state to state to various installations, and he was often absent from home for weeks at a time.

My mother, therefore, was the emotional heart of the family. It was the beginning of the Great Depression and beggars, rag pickers and hobos from passing freights regular-ly made their way through the alley to our back door. Mother would offer them a plate of food and I'd sit on the back stoop talking with them. They were always courteous; there were never any problems.

We lived four blocks from the sylvan paradise of Garfield Park, which was designed by the landscape architect Jens Jensen, who later built the Clearing in Ellison Bay, Wisconsin. The park was a special place for Sunday family picnics, and rental rowboats were available to lazily explore the quiet ponds edged with graceful willows where emerald dragonflies skimmed over the water's surface. I learned to play baseball there, later tennis, and in wintertime when the lagoons became a frozen fairyland, I skated across the ice like a will-of-the-wisp.

I have a distinct memory of my second grade teacher at Ryerson Public School—a frightful woman named Miss Garglin. She was not very big, rather a slim woman but had moles on her face with hairs growing out of them. She was a fanatic about the Palmer method of penmanship. Our daily assignment would be to write a series of letters or sentences over and over again. While clutching a stout ruler in one hand, she'd walk, very slowly, up and down the aisles between our desks. She kept a pair of tweezers in her pocket and every so often she would stop, pluck out a hair, and examine it carefully. Meanwhile, her classroom was absolutely silent; there was no disturbance of any kind. Suddenly, she'd spot an error on someone's paper and "whap!" down came that ruler! Then she'd shout, "This is the worst class I've ever had! Everyone stand up and get into the cloakroom…get into the cloakroom!" The whole class had to file into that dark room and, silently, face the back wall. We remained standing there, penitently, for what seemed to be ages although perhaps it was only five minutes. She was an absolute horror—I never learned anything in her class! Throughout that desolate year I toiled at my desk writing endless sentences while, in the distance, I could hear the mournful whistle of a passing train and I thought, "Oh please God, I have to get out of here! I have to get on that train if it's the last thing I do. It's the only thing I want to do. I have to get on that train and just disappear into the world!"

In contrast to the dreaded Miss Gargin, I fell in love with my first piano teacher—a Miss Bernadene Snyder who was pretty and sweet and smelled good. She was also the preacher's daughter and my Sunday school teacher at Garfield Park Methodist Episcopal Church. I was about eight years old and at lesson time I'd sit next to her on the piano bench happily playing duets together. It was an innocent era, as is evidenced by some of the tunes from my 1927 recital:

"Song of the Bobolink", "The Robin's Secret,"

"The Zephyr Valse," "March of the Goslings,"

"Frolic of the Frogs," and "Airy Fairies."

At that final recital, I happened to glance around at the other people in the room and suddenly realized—I was the only boy there! All the rest of her students were girls! I quit shortly after that.

My best friend was Carl Lervold who lived in the apartment above us. I had a sister named Eleanor who was four years younger than me. I'd play with her, of course, but Carl was my own age and he was a boy. The possibility of daring adventures existed for us on almost a daily basis. We could climb the steep embankment of the Northwestern Railroad to place copper pennies on the steel tracks, or we could go pester the girls who hung out in the courtyard of a neighboring building. They usually wanted to play stupid games like "house." assigning us the male roles of daddy or brother while they were the mommies or sisters. Carl and I, however, preferred to be tough soldiers, so we ended up fighting with the girls instead. Carl was also along when I discovered a little puppy in a neighbor's coal bin. I carried him home with me and bathed him in sudsy water until he came out pure white! I named him "Jack" and he was my best companion for the next 15 years, greeting me joyfully after school and running after sticks in the park.

Carl's mother was from Virginia. She wore a lot of make-up and talked in a slow, melodious voice. She did a lot of soft complaining as she fed us some Southern kind of food—sandwiches with cucumbers and jelly. Her husband had the enviable job of running the big movie projector at the McVickers Theatre in Chicago where Carl and I watched "All Quiet on the Western Front" and "The Big Parade"—no soppy love stories, of course. After school we chased each other through the bushes, fighting with wooden sticks and make-believe guns. We both swore to be brave soldiers: one day we'd fight for our country. Years later, Carl was killed in the South Pacific by the Japanese. I returned from the same war without a scratch.

The Methodist Church was an important part of my family life. My father Alfred Thompson—known in the family as "Tom"—had a resonant baritone voice, spoke with impeccable diction and a slight English accent, and often sang solos in the choir. I remember him playing the role of Judas Iscariot in one of the church pageants, not to mention his thundering speeches on the evils of drink in sobering temperance programs. In the years following World War I patriotic plays were popular, and I played Uncle Sam in a skit called "America," dressed up in a red, white, and blue coat and trousers with a tall hat of stars and stripes.

My father was a rather private person, not comfortable with expressing emotion or sharing his feelings. His father, Edward Mealing Thompson (my grandfather), was British and resembled King George V, wore a three- piece suit, and sported a neatly trimmed beard and moustache. He was born in Brixton, England, trained as a solicitor, and emigrated to California in 1870. I have a photograph dated 1917 of him holding me as an infant surrounded by palm trees. The only other time we met was after my high school graduation in 1934, but he was old and wizened then, and died two years later. My grandfather married Bridget Mary Harrigan in San Francisco in 1882; they had five children, and she died in 1905, years before I was born. My grandmother is an absolute enigma to me because my father never talked about her. She had been born in Sydney, Australia to Irish parents, and whether they were transported there from debtors prison or the potato famine I will never know. Nobody every talked about the circumstances of her death—it was as if she had never existed.

I grew up in an era before television and videos, when families made their own entertainments and every June my father took us to the annual GE picnic that was held in various parks around Chicago. I entered simple games such as the pie eating contest, the three-legged sack race, and various running events; and because I was athletic, I won quite a few prizes. One summer we spent a week's vacation at Norwood Farm on Rush Lake in Hartford, Michigan. City folk like us could rent a cottage or rooms in the farmhouse itself and participate in the farm chores if we wished. It was a working farm with horses, dairy cows, chickens and pigs. We swam in the lake and rowboats were available for fishing. One day I got a fishhook caught in my earlobe. The barb was firmly embedded in the fleshy part and when my parents tried to pry it out with a knife, I fainted. I was only seven or eight.

For me the lake boat excursions from Chicago to Michigan City or Benton Harbor on a hot summer day were as exciting as any ocean voyage. On board were elegant salons that served meals and refreshments, while on deck a lively band played throughout the trip. The ship's weekly arrival was an important event for Michigan City where a carnival atmosphere prevailed, with kiosks selling peanuts, iced drinks, and cotton candy. We were amongst the crush of 600 or so passengers who made a determined dash to the sandy beach to find a spot to spread our blankets and enjoy an afternoon of swimming and sunshine. For me, it was pure Heaven! Another passenger excursion was to Benton Harbor, a slightly more mysterious place. There was a monastery there with a sect of bearded monks, and to my innocent eyes their dark hooded figures seemed rather sinister, as if they belonged to another century or to another world altogether. Their eerie silhouettes gliding noiselessly along, cast a shadow over what was otherwise a brilliant summer day.

It was now 1927 and I was in fifth grade at Ryerson Public School, where the normal Friday after-school activity was playground fighting. It wasn't too serious or particularly dangerous: nobody was really mad at each other. One boy was chosen to fight another, and we were like a bunch of edgy mongrels with their hackles up, just the usual Friday afternoon activity at Ryerson School. The school administration never interfered because they probably knew it wasn't too serious. At the time I was quite a leader: I was cocky, athletic and strong, a bit of a braggart, and I knew how to fight. A boy had squared off to fight me who was about my size but rather flabby, a non-entity really with a pockmarked face. A crowd had gathered around us and I remember my friends shouting, "O.K. Rob, go get him! Go after him now, Rob!" But within minutes I was flat on the ground. He landed a punch that almost knocked me out!

I attribute a change in my personality to this fight. I had always been rather self-confident, feeling I could handle anything, but it was now clearly evident that I could be beaten. A daunting realization! As a result, I became more introspective, more self-doubting, and more self-conscious.

My mother, always concerned about our health and well-being, decided it was now time to move to the suburbs where the air was fresher and the schools were better. We moved to Villa Park.

Chapter 2
Villa Park

We moved to Villa Park in 1927 where there was a feeling of open spaces, and the nearby farmland reminded my mother of growing up in the country in western Illinois and Iowa. Villa Park was the poor sister to the neighboring suburbs of Elmhurst and Lombard; and, of course, Wheaton and Glen Ellyn were wealthier still. It was right on the Chicago-Aurora-Elgin electric line, so convenient to my father's office in the Loop. At first we lived in a rather terrible house on Ardmore Avenue with floods in the basement, but within months we had moved to a nicer home on Harvard Avenue with better neighbors and more yard for my dog Jack to play in.

At this time we took a rather permanent boarder into our home, my flamboyant Aunt Faye Van Der Veer, my mother's worldly younger sister. She worked as a stenographer to Admiral Byrd, the Arctic explorer, and in 1928 she traveled to Europe by herself on the ocean liner, *The S.S. DeGrasse*. She had flown in airplanes and had boyfriends who took her dancing at fancy places like the Palmer House or the Drake Hotel. Her hair was flaming red, she wore make-up, a stylish hat and a red fox flung across her shoulders, and had the substantial figure of a Gibson girl! An imposing woman with her platform shoes and ankle straps, she was almost six feet tall, a legacy from her father Tunis Van Der Veer who was a stout farmer of Dutch origins. Aunt Faye had dated my father originally, but I think she was too high-spirited for him, so he married my mother instead. Faye enjoyed everything about life: she threw parties at the drop of a hat for whatever occasion, and her unbridled laughter was like a scream of joy. She lavished affection upon my sister, Eleanor, and me, often smothering us with kisses. She had been married once to a Thomas Coyne, but soon found out he was a drunkard and left him after a week. In fact she was the exact opposite of my mother, who was a plain Christian woman without much charm or beauty. My mother had helped raise Faye, who was eleven years younger. They were always very compatible and it seemed only natural that, with my father away on business much of the time, Aunt Faye made her home with us.

At about this time Aunt Faye decided that it was imperative that I learn how to dance, so she took me to the Palmer House where her favorite ensemble, the Wayne King Orchestra, was playing. She was a powerful woman and quick on her feet. With a resolute grip on my waist and counting "one-two-three, one-two-three" she pushed me backwards and forwards across the parquet. I was clumsy and felt hot with embarrassment but Aunt Faye was more determined than I was, so we lurched around the ballroom several times more. She was also concerned that Eleanor and I know how to behave in proper society with credible table manners and correct etiquette, and through Aunt Faye we were exposed to the hitherto unknown world of beautiful clothes, sophistication and glamour. She was always dating some guy who had money, and we were sometimes taken along to the Pump Room at the Ambassador East Hotel or the Edgewater Beach Hotel where we heard the big bands of Paul Whiteman or Tommy Dorsey play.

It was during this period that I learned that Aunt Faye had a close friend named Josephine Russell, who just happened to be the cousin of Tom Mix. Oh my God, Tom Mix, my absolute hero whom I'd watched, countless times, gallop across the screen on his horse Tony! My Aunt knew someone who was related to Tom Mix! It was like being related to royalty!! From that moment on, Aunt Faye rose sky-high in my estimation!

When we joined the Westmore Methodist Church my mother finally found her spiritual home. The church was just in the next village, not far from our house, and the nice young couple, Pastor Sidney Bloomquist and his wife Mary, had recently moved there from Iowa. My mother practically adopted them! Pastor Bloomquist was very down to earth, a friend to everyone in the congregation, and they became lifelong friends of my parents. My father was active in the church and tithed regularly, yet his attitude towards religion puzzled me. He often joked that although he had some doubts about God and Jesus Christ, nevertheless "it was always better to be on the safe side and to believe." My father was a Knights Templar and Mason, and as there were various secret rituals involved, I always assumed that this was the reason he had never formally joined the Methodist Church. It was only after his death in 1950 that I was shocked to learn from a family friend that he had been raised Catholic! His mother, Bridget Mary Harrigan Thompson, had sent him to Catholic schools. For me, it was just the final example of how little he shared about his early life, which for me would be forever veiled in mystery!

My mother, on the other hand, lived her religion. The country was now deep in the Depression. I remember how one of our neighbors, a man who had had quite a good job, a nice house and family, was now selling apples door to door in the street. Fortunately, my father had steady employment at GE and we were never seriously affected by the Depression. Through her church connections, my mother sometimes took in girls who had "gotten in trouble" and cared for them until they were able to get back on their feet again. She was always helping people. Later, when we had moved to Downers Grove, there was an elderly lady, Mrs. Roll, who lived across the street from us. When she took sick and had no savings, my mother paid the doctor's bills. She called up his office and said, "Please send the bill to me." That was the way she was; it was her small town farming community upbringing where neighbors helped each other.

If someone was sick, you brought food and offered to help. People took care of each other.

My mother's handsome nephew, Don Cave, had a well-known band called the Melody Five, which played in vaudeville on the Orpheum circuit during the 1920's. We would drive out to St. Charles to the Baker Hotel on the Fox River to watch them perform. The tobacco heiress Doris Duke had something to do with the ownership of the hotel, and rumor had it that she had been in love with Don and had at one time wanted to marry him. Of course, this was all prior to his marriage to Margit Hegedus, the gifted "gypsy violinist" from Hungary.

The drive to St. Charles took several hours over bad roads, and it was a lucky day when our 1927 Dodge had only two flat tires along the way. There were a lot of arguments on these trips. Actually, my mother was a better driver than my father—he had difficulty with the gears and his eyesight was not that good—so road trips were often fraught with marital tensions.

Margit Hegedus and her sister were classically trained violinists from the Budapest Conservatory. The impresario who "discovered" them promised them a brilliant career in America, but failed to meet their boat when it docked in New York. Stranded there with no money and little knowledge of English, they found jobs in vaudeville. The venue was usually a silent movie, then a series of musical comedy acts like Sophie Tucker, Jack Benny or Eddie Cantor. Margit and her gypsy violin might follow one of the dog acts. Later, she made her way to Chicago where she performed on radio and at elegant restaurants in the Palmer House or Drake Hotel. It was there that Jascha Heifetz heard her play and commented that she was far too gifted a violinist to be appearing in vaudeville.

Don Cave and Margit moved to California in the 1930's where he became a successful musical agent booking dance bands throughout the country. Every Monday night we would listen to the Grace Moore Show broadcast live from the Hollywood Bowl and featuring Margit Hegedus, a soloist with the Raymond Page Orchestra. She and Don performed at the Coconut Grove and the Hotel Del Coronado and they lived on a Los Angeles ranch where their closest neighbor was Dennis Day.

I was now in 7th or 8th grade at Ardmore School, and as part of science class they taught a subject call "Hygiene" which was actually the tepid equivalent of modern day sex education. I thought the class unnecessary and rather personal compared to what I believed was really essential—math, history, English and science. At that time, my major interest in Villa Park was scouting; nothing was so satisfying. C.R. Fogg was our scoutmaster at Calvary Evangelical Church, and as honest and trustworthy a man as you could ever hope for. He was Canadian and a role model for me. I had determined by now that my goal in life was to be a sea captain in the Merchant Marines. If I were going to sea, I needed a boat, of course. I was taking Industrial Arts at school, so I already knew how to work with tools. To earn a scout merit badge, I designed a kayak which was rather sleek, made of thin planking, proper gunnels and thwarts, and was covered with canvas—in all, it was about 2 feet wide and 12 feet in length and decorated with the good luck symbol of the Native Americans, unfortunately the swastika. When it was finished, we took the kayak to be launched in a small lake near Wheaton. I must have already had a tendency towards the theatric because I prefaced the actual launching with a few ceremonial taps on my bugle. Then, with the entire scout troop watching, I put one leg into the kayak and pushed off from shore. I was only about four feet into the lake when the boat flipped over—it was a total disaster! The kayak was so top heavy that it was completely unstable, and eventually I had to build outriggers to keep it from capsizing again!

Outside of scouts, I was quite unaware of people in general. In 1930 I started my freshman year at York High School in Elmhurst. I rode my bicycle there, a distance of about two miles along the only road connecting the two towns, the St. Charles Road. My four years at high school were singularly unremarkable—I never made honor roll, never played on an athletic team, was never called to the Principal's office, never flunked a course, and I was already in my junior year when I suddenly became aware that I was the only one in school still wearing short pants or knickerbockers—all the other boys were wearing long pants!

The only time I received an A was from my Latin teacher, Miss Lois Ashton. She had come to Chicago from a farming community in southern Indiana, and as she was alone and new to the city, my kind-hearted mother had thought to include her in all our holiday dinners at Thanksgiving, Christmas and Easter. Consequently, when school got out that summer, Miss Ashton invited me to visit her folks' farm in North Vernon, Indiana for two weeks. It was June 1931, in the midst of the Depression, and there were few summer jobs available for boys my age. I imagined a farm visit would probably be rather boring, but as I had nothing better to do at the time, I decided I might as well go.

I arrived in North Vernon by train dressed in my Sunday knickers and cap, and carrying my suitcase. I was met by Miss Ashton, who drove us over hot dusty roads to the farm twelve miles away. Her parents were Will and Alice Ashton, and during that first week I learned about farm chores. Tuesday was wash day; it was my job to build a fire under the big black iron kettle in the backyard to heat up the water. I began the day at 4:30 a.m. milking the dairy cows, crouching beneath them balanced on a three-legged stool. When I was finally able to squeeze a steady stream from the udder and make froth in the bucket, I was enormously pleased with myself. After milking, Mrs. Ashton served us a monumental breakfast of pancakes with home-canned meat.

She cooked and canned almost constantly and had a vast vegetable garden that I tended, row upon unending row. In the fields there was tobacco that needed to be harvested and hung in the barn to dry, while the eggs needed to be gathered from the henhouse. But it wasn't all work; I had fun too, riding bareback on "Old Bell", the big white farm horse, or going swimming in the Muscatatuck River with Miss Ashton's two brothers, James and Roger.

Their father, Will Ashton, was a retired schoolteacher. A lean fellow, he looked ageless. I can still see him now, loping across the farmyard in his slouched, shambly gait. He could work from sunup 'til sundown and then get up early the next morning to do it all over again. He was tireless! It was only on Sundays that he allowed himself a day of rest, and then he lounged around the kitchen in a clean pair of overalls, telling stories. We attended the Tea Creek Baptist Church where members were baptized by immersion in the creek itself.

All too soon my time on the farm grew short; the second week was almost over and sadly, I'd have to go back home again. One morning after breakfast, Mrs. Ashton said to me, "Rob, if you would like to stay longer, you're welcome to do so." That was music to my ears and I ended up staying the rest of the summer! During those weeks a fourteen-year-old city boy was slowly being transformed into a country boy. I dressed in bib overalls; my bare feet became so tough that the stones didn't hurt. I shot squirrels and discovered that the meat was as tasty as chicken, and I could save the skin and mount it for my taxidermy merit badge in scouting. I got to help Uncle Ernest take a load of cows and pigs to market in Columbus. I'd hang out at our neighbor Wash Kinder's farm and listen to the old-timer spin yarns. One evening, one of the Ashton cousins, Pete, arranged a date for me with a buxom farm girl. She sat in one corner of the back seat and I sat in the other, and when Pete deliberately swerved the car by making sharp turns at high speed, we'd fall against each other. Very exciting! At the end of the seven weeks, I arrived back at Chicago's Union Station dressed in bib overalls, straw hat, barefoot, with a tanned squirrel skin in a corked bottle in my suitcase. I had become a genuine farm hick! Thereafter, throughout my remaining years of high school, I returned to the Ashton's every summer. I loved it!!

My mother's closest friend, an old schoolmate from Burlington, Iowa named "Aunt Grace" Hunt now lived in Maywood. We called her "Aunt Grace" because she and her husband had no children, and they more or less adopted my sister Eleanor and me as their own. A weekend visit to Maywood was a breath of fresh air for my mother and me, not only because of the delectable lemon meringue pies, but also because the Des Plaines River was just two blocks away. You could rent canoes there, and in 1933 or so I bought one for $30. I named it "The Driftwood." It was a whitewater canoe with a reinforced metal keel and an enclosed bow, half-ribbed for strength. It was very stable and almost unsinkable! For an extra $5 they threw in a backrest and a sail. A canoe was the love machine of the 1920's and 1930's! You were too young to drive, you didn't have a car, but you could take a girl out canoeing. I was a boy scout so I knew quite a bit about canoeing and water safety—less about girls, though.

Each year York High School sponsored an annual talent show. I had played the guitar for several years now, self-taught really, and once I'd mastered the basic chords I was able to play quite a number of songs. For years I had entertained at scout meetings with my very fat friend Bob Howden, and we both believed we possessed hidden musical talent. I was a fan of Gene Autry—his songs were easy to play and they told a story—so for talent night I decided to perform a version of "My Cross-Eyed Gal." Dressed in full western regalia of cowboy hat, boots, shirt, jeans and bolo tie, I mounted the stage and began to sing:

"Oh, she's done gone away, kicked the bucket yesterday.
My cross-eyed gal who lived upon the hill.
She took strychnine and died, and I hope she's satisfied
'cuz she did the whole durn thing against my will!"

And then I yodeled! I was really getting into the part and in my mind I had become Gene Autry—my hero! The audience seemed to be enjoying it so I repeated a verse and, with mounting enthusiasm, I yodeled some more. Cheers and wild applause greeted me when I took my final bow, and it was only afterwards that I learned that our very dignified Superintendent of Schools, Mr. George C. Letts, had fallen off his chair with laughter. Apparently, my ridiculous sincerity combined with my immoderate yodeling had finished him off. My performance that night became the stuff of school legend!

As you may have surmised by now, I was still quite naïve about girls at this point. My Aunt Faye had tried valiantly, but to no avail, to teach me to dance. A souvenir from her 1928 voyage to Europe was a program from the Folies Bergère which contained naughty photographs of nude women dancing with tassels on their breasts. Now and then I'd sneak it out of her bedroom to examine the pictures. It was now junior prom time and I was much too shy to risk asking a girl for a date. I remember attending the prom with Ralph Swarner—another poor, miserable creature like myself—both identically dressed in formal white coats with neatly pressed blue trousers. We sat together in the balcony of the high school gymnasium and watched the couples dancing below us, all the while making snide comments about the girls like—"Heh, that one's really sexy!" or "Look at that fat little blimp!"

At that time I was unaware of life and completely absorbed in my dream of becoming a sea captain. To that end I was taking math, science, physics and chemistry classes. I was an Eagle Scout now and I longed for adventure. I was going to travel the Seven Seas and see the world!

Then an event took place that radically altered my course in life. It's possible that the gypsies had found me after all, and had returned to steal me away. This sudden change materialized in the guise of my English teacher, Miss Tekla Wainio. From the beginning, I was intrigued by her unusual name and her theatrical air. Whether it was her voice, the angle of her hat, or the cut of her stylish maroon suit, she looked like an actress to me. Senior year we were required to take public speaking, followed by a class in oral interpretation that consisted of reading passages out loud from Shakespeare, the Bible, poetry and other literature. Suddenly, I discovered that I had the ability, by using my imagination, to interpret the characters of Hamlet, Macbeth, and Shylock and to give a convincing portrayal of them. Miss Wainio praised my narration and gave me extra encouragement. Through her guidance and inspiration I discovered, at last, something I was suited for—I had found my niche! All that was required was that I use what I already possessed— a deep resonant voice, my imagination, a quick mind, and a strong desire to succeed. Acting was something I could do, something I would never grow tired of. I had always assumed that famous actors or movie stars were just born that way. I never realized that you could study for the theatre. When I learned that there were schools like the Goodman in Chicago or other theatre schools out East where you could learn to act, it occurred to me that maybe I didn't have to become a sea captain after all. I was struggling with math and physics anyway; in comparison, acting came easily to me. It was almost second nature.

Miss Wainio cast me in my first character role as Herbert Dean in the play about the famous Barrymore family called "The Royal Family." Now, when I studied my face in the mirror, I thought I could detect a very definite resemblance to my new hero—John Barrymore!

Chapter 3
The Gypsies Take Me

Where do you go to college when your grades aren't brilliant but only rather mediocre? I had no possibility of a scholarship. In May 1934 we had moved to Downers Grove. The nearest school was in Naperville, a small Christian college called North Central where the tuition was $85 a semester and I could live at home.

My theatre professor was Guy Oliver, the old orator. A short, balding man, he and his wife used to perform Shakespeare readings at ladies' book clubs. His training came from the old school of acting, the 1890's period, where actors relied on dramatic oratory and exaggerated gestures to portray their characters. Years before, he had actually directed my father in a few of the Methodist Church pageants. However, the old school had now been supplanted by the Stanislavsky method from the Moscow Art Theatre, which stressed realism rather than exaggeration. Stanislavsky believed the actor should immerse himself in the character of the role, assuming the very identity of the part. In addition to theatre classes, I took geology, French, English, and Bible studies, and for the first time in my schooling I got "A's"! It all seemed to make sense now. During the next two years, I performed in plays at North Central's Pfeiffer Hall and, by a fluke, was elected Junior Class President!

It happened this way: I had recently appeared as Benedict, Lord of Padua, in *Much Ado About Nothing* and from it had achieved a certain notoriety on campus. During the election for class president, the two top candidates (both football heroes, no doubt!) were tied in a dead heat each time the ballot was cast. So while fumbling around trying to come up with another nominee, somehow my name must have been mentioned—they had all seen me in the play. I won by default, so to speak.

Besides being elected class president for my junior year, Professor Oliver had asked me to become his speech assistant, a position that paid a small stipend. I realized I needed to learn more about theatre—up until now all I knew had come from Professor Oliver and Tekla Wainio—so I did some research into summer stock and found out that on the East Coast there were the Ogunquit Playhouse, Cape Dennis, Cape May and Berkshire Playhouses. I wrote letters of inquiry to most of them and discovered they were quite expensive and did not offer scholarships. Then I found the Duluth Summer School of Theatre. It offered six weeks of training, was not so far from Chicago, and cost $150. Their brochure stated that they had a distinguished faculty drawn from Northwestern University, Boston Academy, and Dr. Maurice Gnesin, the Director of the Goodman Theatre School. I decided that this school offered everything that I needed at this point.

In the summer of 1936, I took the train to Duluth, Minnesota. I had arranged to board with the Luddens who were somehow connected with the school. John Wray Young, who was the head of the school, taught acting and directing while his wife taught costuming. The tall and very distinguished Juliet Barker from Northwestern taught voice and diction, and Ivard Strauss of Boston Academy, the author of that veritable lexicon for aspiring actors, *Paint, Powder and Make-up*, taught theatre history. He taught me everything I needed to know about make-up: how an actor could play any character, from youth to ancient crone, all through the appropriate application of make-up, wigs and costumes. Throughout my sixty-year career in the theatre, I've always done my own make-up. Of course, for some time now I haven't needed make-up to appear older, I'm already old!

During the final two weeks of that summer I was cast as the juvenile lead in the play *Accent on Youth* by Samson Raphaelson. At the close of the season, Dr. Gnesin called me into his office. He was a rather severe individual and spoke with a precise Russian accent. "Mr. Thompson, I think it may all be moonshine, but I think you will make an actor. Would you like to come to the Goodman Theatre on a scholarship?" (Between each of these phrases he would pause first and then suck in his breath. I think his teeth were not very good.) After he had finished, he said, "Just let me know."

I left his office in a daze, "Just let me know…let me know." His last phrase resonated through my brain and I thought "My God in heaven, I'm going to need some help with this decision," so I decided to go down to the shore of Lake Superior in order to think. I needed to deliberate in peaceful surroundings and I needed to talk to God. I pleaded with him: "God, you have to tell me what to do, please let me know what I should do!" After several hours of meditation, it became clear to me that he was telling me to "Go to the Goodman, go to the Goodman Theatre!" So I had to write to Professor Oliver to tell him that I wouldn't be returning to North Central, and I had to notify the school that I would not be accepting the presidency of the junior class.

Chapter 4
Goodman Theatre School

It's my first day at the Goodman and I was part of a group of 30 or 40 new students milling around the lobby while waiting to descend into the Kenneth Sawyer Goodman Memorial Theatre for orientation. I glanced around, sizing up my classmates, two thirds of which were male, and came to the conclusion that with the exception of a few students, nobody really looked like an actor, like the people I had seen in the movies. Most, in fact, looked rather ordinary, and I felt somewhat smug knowing that I had received a personal invitation from the Director to attend the Goodman Theatre School.

Once the orientation was completed, I quickly sought out Dr. Gnesin's private office located at the end of the great hall. His secretary was a young, blonde woman named Miss Irene Foget. I breezed right past her desk as I was just going to pop into his office to say a brief hello. When I opened his door, I was confronted by a very formal Dr. Gnesin who advised me never to enter his office again without Miss Foget's explicit permission. This curt and quite unexpected response deflated my ego somewhat.

The training I received while at the Goodman was of the highest quality and had a profound influence on my later career. Mary Agnes Doyle, an actress originally from the Abbey Theatre in Dublin, was my most distinguished teacher. She resembled Maude Adams or Charlotte Cushman and favored gowns of the previous century with a little cape affect at the shoulders. These gowns were of muted colors; either dove gray, green or a deep claret, which fell all the way to the floor—you never saw any suggestion of an ankle or a leg. Miss Doyle instructed us in voice and diction: an actor must know how to enunciate every syllable and, above all, know how to breathe correctly from the diaphragm and not just through the mouth. Her daily dozen diction drills were designed to eliminate our flat Midwestern nasal twang. She previewed every play we performed to critique our diction, and afterwards, sent us detailed notes with her comments and corrections.

One year I was given the role of "Old Chris" in Eugene O'Neill's *Anna Christie* (Lionel Barrymore had played the role in the movie version which starred Greta Garbo). It was a challenge for me as a young actor and I was having difficulty finding my character, even up to the time of the dress rehearsal. It was only when I put on the costume with the heavy boots, I suddenly discovered how Old Chris might walk, and I was finally able to assume his character. Later, it meant a great deal to me when Miss Doyle commented in class, "You should watch Robert Thompson—he is Old Chris from his feet up, from his toes to his head!" For me, it was wonderful praise, especially because it came from her. I remember once disagreeing with her suggestion that Old Chris needed to speak more distinctly. I countered with, "I just can't do that, Miss Doyle, because this gruff old sailor would be more likely to mutter or mumble at his age." I thought she might be offended and perhaps never speak to me again, but over the four years I was at the Goodman, we became very delightful friends and later she wrote kind letters of introduction for me to her New York friends who were connected with the theatre.

Another wonderful teacher of mine was David B. Itken, formerly an actor with the Habima Theatre in Moscow. He was a heavy-set fellow with wild hair, passionate emotions, and a strong Russian accent. One of his daughters, Bella Itken, later became a well-known acting teacher at the Goodman when it had moved to De Paul University. I learned Stanislavsky from him, which was first to act out the role in pantomime, and, above all, to imbue the part with genuine emotion. I can hear Itken now, his voice rising in a fiery crescendo, "You must build the character, build the character...!" I understood completely what he was trying to convey to us, and he cast me in every show that he directed during my four years at school. More than once, he would say to our class, "Watch Thompson, just watch Thompson, he makes the stage *burn*!" (That final word rumbled out of him like some unexpected volcano.) While still a first year student, I was cast as a clown in *The Winter's Tale* by Shakespeare. The lead role of Leontes, the King of Sicily, was played by the very brilliant Mladin Secoulevich, who later became the actor Karl Malden. He was two years ahead of me; and Sam Wanamaker, later of the Globe Theatre, was between us. I acted with Sam Wanamaker many times, both at the Goodman and the Peninsula Players.

Charlotte Chorpenning was another special teacher who wrote and directed highly imaginative and enchanting adaptations of children's plays like *Prince and the Pauper*, *Alice in Wonderland*, and *Rumpelstiltskin*, which were performed every Saturday afternoon by the beginning acting students. "Chorpy", as she was affectionately known, had the shape of a stout chef in an ample kitchen, but when demonstrating a character for us, could easily transform herself into a marching soldier or an elf. Children's plays were an excellent training ground for us to develop our timing and our characterization skills because if we weren't sharp or dramatic enough, children tended to get restless and began to squirm around in their seats.

The Director of the Goodman, the eminent Dr. Maurice Gnesin, had an intellectual and more mechanical approach to acting as compared to David Itkin's highly emotional methods, so perhaps the combination of the two Russians provided a balance for us beginning actors who were struggling to learn our craft. Dr. Gnesin always treated me in a formal manner and usually criticized every scene I ever did in class or on stage, much more than I thought I deserved. He frequently would preface these comments with, "Mr. Thompson, if you wish to remain in the Goodman Theatre program..." followed by his current criticism.

One incident that I have never forgotten occurred during a type of oral examination. Every six weeks we were required to prepare a scene, and at the end of the first year a final scene, which, if performed successfully, would allow you to return to the Goodman for the second year. I remember being on stage and doing my scene with some girl whose name I've forgotten. David Itken, Mary Agnes Doyle and Dr. Gnesin were amongst those in the audience evaluating our performance. My scene was very dramatic and I became so emotionally involved that I began to cry—it was a very heavy scene. When we were finished, we sat down and anxiously awaited their comments. Several moments of silence went by and I began to feel, "My God, I was good in that part; I was tremendous!" I imagined that they probably were going to advise me not to even bother continuing at the Goodman but to go straight to Broadway instead—or perhaps even to Hollywood! I could hear them now saying, "We have nothing more to teach you, my dear Mr. Thompson, you were so outstanding!" After several more minutes of silence, Dr. Gnesin merely commented, "Mr. Thompson...the object of acting is to make the audience cry... not yourself!"

It was at the Goodman that I had my first taste of performing on radio in weekly broadcast of student plays adapted to a half hour time slot. Later, in my final years, I played bit parts in NBC soap operas like *Helen Trent*, *Bob Becker*, or *The Trouble with Marriage*. I was paid $15 for the rehearsal and $30 for the actual program itself. In 1938 and 1939 this was very big money indeed! I also appeared regularly as *Dr. Lawrence* for the Chicago Dental Society on WGN Radio, a fifteen-minute spot every Friday afternoon for which I was paid $5. *Dr. Lawrence* (me) would answer questions about dental care presumably mailed in by the public but actually written by my own Downers Grove dentist. The show would run until baseball season, when it was supplanted by Chicago Cubs coverage. It would resume again in the fall, once baseball season was over.

Because I had shown promise, I was invited back for a fourth year at the Goodman on a working scholarship. This entailed, in addition to all my classroom work, that I be available to work backstage or to usher when performances, dance recitals, lectures, slide shows, or meetings were held at the theatre. It was often past midnight when I finally returned home to Downers Grove, and sometimes I missed the last train. Then, of course, I'd have to get up early again the next morning to attend classes, so I found a room in the Eastgate Hotel on Ohio and Michigan for $3 a week.

Above the ornately carved proscenium of the Goodman stage is the motto: *You yourself must set fire to the faggots you have brought.* This was ostensibly an admonition for the theatre audience to leave behind any preconceptions and be open, instead, to whatever was presented here. In moments of tedium, as we students lolled around in our seats during lectures, we would occasionally glance up at that inscription and snicker. It was a very innocent era and I only gradually realized that "faggots" had a meaning other than pieces of kindling wood—that there were boys who liked boys rather than girls. Sometime later, I dated a girl named Muriel with whom I hoped to form a famous acting team like the Lunts, but in the end, she wasn't that interested.

It was during this time that another classmate, Roger Tracy, was dating a rather large girl whose most compelling attraction was that she had a very rich grandmother who lived at the Ambassador East Hotel. The four of us were able to dine there in the elegant Pump Room where we could order anything on the menu, and later she would sign her grandmother's name to the bill. Roger, of course, clung to this girl like a limpet, and fortunately their relationship lasted for almost a year.

The Pump Room was a mecca for the rich and famous and I remember one night when all my illusions were shattered. John Barrymore who was in town starring in *My Dear Children* was sitting in a booth nearby. When he staggered to his feet to leave, I was shocked to see that he was old, paunchy, rather short and drunk as a coot! What a sad ending to a magnificent career! In my years at the Goodman, I saw many of the great actors of that era perform at the Erlanger, Selwyn, Harris, Shubert, or Blackstone theatres: Walter Hampton, John Gielgud, Eva Le Gallienne, Leslie Howard, Maurice Evans, and perhaps the greatest and most thrilling of all—Lawrence Olivier, Vivien Leigh and Dame Mae Whitty perform in *Romeo and Juliet*! Of course, my seats were so far back in the upper balcony that the stage looked like a postage stamp and the actors like tiny puppets!

In 1938, while still a student at the Goodman, I was asked to act with the Peninsula Players, a summer stock theatre in Fish Creek, Wisconsin, founded by the Fisher family. And so began my love affair with the Players, which continues even today after 65 years.

Chapter 5

Peninsula Players 1938–39

In the early days of the Peninsula Players, Caroline Fisher would contact theatre schools such as Madison, Northwestern and the Goodman looking for promising young actors who were willing to work for $5 a week plus room and board. When I mentioned to my father that I would be acting at the Players, which was owned by the Fisher family, he seemed quite pleased because, in fact, he already knew Caroline's father, C. R. Fisher, an electrical genius who had designed and patented the mammoth conveyor apparatus used by US Steel to load gravel and shale into ore boats at Rogers City, Michigan on Lake Huron. One of my father's co-workers at GE, a man named Sanborn, was familiar with Door County and offered to drive me up there. On the way we stopped at Smith Brothers Fish Shanty in Port Washington for one of their delicious 35 cent fish sandwiches.

The Peninsula Players first season in 1935 had been performed *en plein air* in the sloping garden behind the home of Mrs. Hedwiga Welcker Brigl, later the site of the Bonnie Brook Motel in Fish Creek. However, the following year the Fisher family had purchased the former Wildwood Boy's Camp, a pristine 20 acre tract along the shores of Green Bay, and spent the summer of 1936 building the theatre and making improvements to the property. When I arrived in 1938 there were just four buildings: the theatre, the lodge, the dormitory, and the boathouse with a pier and diving raft. There were also very few trees compared with what there are today. We actors slept in a four-bedroom dormitory that housed 16 people: there were two bunk beds in each bedroom, leaving very little space for clothing, suitcases or trunks. The plumbing arrangements were not quite finalized, so the baths we took those first few days consisted of dips in the lake. For us neophyte actors the possibility of living and breathing theatre for twenty-four hours a day was a heady experience. It was an art theatre and the play selection in those early years was dazzling: classic plays by Noel Coward, Henrik Ibsen, Oscar Wilde, Sophocles and others.

But my strongest memories were of the Fisher family themselves whose creative vision shaped what the Peninsula Players is today, 65 years later. In 1938, Caroline Fisher was only twenty-four, yet at that comparatively young age she already possessed the personality and public relation skills of a budding impresario. She had immense volatility and vivacity, an exuberance for life, beguiling charisma—she absolutely captivated people! She had little difficulty convincing local businessmen, lawyers, bankers and resort owners that, with their support, the theatre could benefit not only tourism but the community as a whole. The Theatre in the Garden would lend an air of distinction to the county, a certain cachet. After all, there was no other form of entertainment at that time: no Peninsula Music Festival, Birch Creek nor American Folklore Theatre. With the exception of a lone movie theatre in Sturgeon Bay, the Peninsula Players was it!

Caroline, a striking brunette, was one of Chicago's leading models working, at that time, at Saks Fifth Avenue. She was a favorite of the famous fashion photographer of the 1930's and 1940's, Valentine Sarra, who was also infatuated with her. She once commented that "He's the only man I've ever driven with to Door County who never got out of second gear!" (A talent for photography does not necessarily a competent driver make.)

One day while modeling at Saks, she was "discovered" by the Hollywood producer, Wesley Ruggles. She went to

Hollywood under special contract with Metro-Goldwyn-Mayer where she trained with other baby starlets who were being taught acting, studio diction and working before the camera. She was extremely photogenic and this, combined with her natural vivacity and lack of inhibition, would have made her suitable for any number of parts, but she was not a dramatic actress, nor did she ever claim to be. While at the Peninsula Players her theatrical skills were more a matter of bluff, bluster and volume, but she looked marvelous, her costumes were exquisite and, most important, the audience loved her—she exuded glamour!

Caroline and her brother Richard were rather precocious children. Richard entered Northwestern University at 15 and he was only 20 when his parents, C. R. and Lydia Fisher, started the theatre. "Richie" was very much the brilliant boy genius who was passionate about writing, directing and producing plays mainly as vehicles for his two beautiful sisters, Caroline and Margot. The final play of the season was always a satirical musical revue that Richie would write in collaboration with Helen Bragdon, a fine character actress and Caroline's assistant for twenty years. At times, the literary and political content of these satires was way over my head. I found some of the humor baffling, yet the relatively sophisticated audiences seemed to enjoy them. Richie lent his creative genius to the Players for many years, but he later moved on to Hollywood, working with CBS-TV as head of production of the Burns and Allen Show, and assistant director of the Jack Benny Show.

The Players began with very lofty ideals. A quote from their 1939 booklet, penned no doubt by Richie, intoned that:

> *"Three thousand years ago in ancient Greece the theatre was born out of the Dionysian and the Bacchanalian wine festivals. The theatre was born of the human reverence for pageantry, dance, and song out-of-doors.*

*The Peninsula Players endeavor to bring the theatre
back to its rightful heritage. The wildness is gone…Bacchus,
the god of revelry has faded into Mythology…but the theatre
is immortal and will live always."*

Caroline and Richard's grand vision of a summer theatre could not have been realized without the financial support and continued involvement of their parents, C. R. and Lydia Fisher, who were also blessed with intellect, abundant energy and a passion for the theatre.

Lydia Fisher (everyone called her "Mama") was probably in her late forties when I first met her. She was plump in the manner of Victorian ladies, and favored a lace jabot or ruffles at the neckline. Originally from Silesia, we affectionately called her "the mad Prussian." She was very motherly to all of us but also quite strict. She was a marvelous cook, somehow producing three meals a day on a huge wood-fired stove for the twenty-five or so members of the theatre colony. She grew some of the produce in her own vegetable garden nearby, and was adamant that we young people have enough to eat, urging us to empty our plates. Besides being a cook and gardener, she had a degree in fashion design from Pratt Institute in New York and sewed the most imaginative costumes for all the productions. I'll never forget that first day I arrived at the Players and heard the music of Wagner filtering through the pine trees. Mama Fisher adored music and opera, owned a Capehart which, at that time, was the Cadillac of sound equipment. It had a huge console with speakers and could play a complete stack of 78 rpm records. The Fishers had an extensive classical music collection of Mozart, Tchaikovsky, Strauss, and many others, which was delightful to listen to, especially on cold, rainy days when we enjoyed relaxing around the cozy fireplace in the lodge.

The Fishers had a wide circle of German-American friends who supported the theatre: the Apfelbachs, the Buchbinders, the Hackmeisters, the Friedmans, the

Welckers, and Freda and Edward Collins. A fairly regular visitor from Chicago during the 1938-39 seasons was a handsome Austrian named Corte Streib (originally Kurt Streib) who sold Jacqueline Cochran make-up for the famous female aviator of the same name. Mr. Streib possessed a certain mature look and, combined with his abundant wavy hair, I'm sure every woman in the world would have loved to have had an affair with him. The minute he set foot on the property, Mama Fisher would put Richard Tauber on the Capehart and the inviting strains of German lieder would waft through the woods. She'd quickly smooth her hair, apply fresh lipstick and waltz out to welcome him. Mama Fisher and Corte had a true affinity for each other. She was devoted to her husband, but C. R. Fisher was otherworldly, his mind often focused on grappling with some arcane electrical problem to do with the theatre.

C. R. Fisher, originally from Boston, was a marine engineer who designed electrical systems for large ships, and through government contracts had met Leathem Smith of Sturgeon Bay who introduced him to Door County's natural beauty. At the Players he was responsible for the theatre's lighting equipment, but was also the general factotum in charge of building and plumbing maintenance. He was tall, lanky and balding, and occasionally he could be persuaded to perform in minor roles when he would be listed in the playbill by his stage name, "C. Raeburn Fyfe". He had a marvelous profile, prominent nose with strong jaw-line and, therefore, looked very distinguished on stage. Because he was a genius, he often did not pay attention to mundane things. I remember sitting at his table during mealtimes where he'd be absentmindedly stirring his coffee, his mind a million light years away, and meanwhile his coffee was overflowing the saucer onto the table. Mama would look over and exclaim, "Papa, you're spilling your coffee again," and as if awakening from some distant dream, he'd mumble, "Whaa...oh...ah...well, so what if I am!"

There have always been bats living at the Peninsula Players, but in those early years there were far more than there are today. C. R. spent an inordinate amount of time pondering the bat problem. During the evening performances they always gravitated towards the stage lights, and although C. R. had strung a maze of wires above the stage, that didn't seem to have the least affect on the bats who were just as blatant and numerous as ever. He was now formulating a scheme to capture the bats. I once overhead him pontificating to some captive listeners, "You know that scientists have analyzed the components in bat's milk. Bats, although winged, are tiny mammals and they suckle their young. I have reached the conclusion that bat milk is of a superior quality in terms of vitamins, minerals and other lactose elements. If only we could capture them and milk them for commercial purposes, we would have a profitable enterprise!" His enthusiasm for this scheme was so convincing that, after a while, his audience began to believe in his theories, remarking, "Golly, if the milk is that valuable, it sounds like something we should get involved with!" In many ways, C. R. was quite a character but, in my mind, his obsession with domesticating bats was the epitome of dottiness!!

Caroline's lovely younger sister, Margot, was just 18 my first summer at the Players. She knew almost nothing about acting then, but she had a voluptuous body that could have driven most men to distraction. She was starring in Oscar Wilde's play, *Salome,* and I was John the Baptist. They had made a plaster cast of my head with straws sticking out of my nose so I could breathe. When the cast was finished, it was covered with long hair to resemble the gruesome severed head of John the Baptist, to be carried on stage at the end of the play on a tray. Meanwhile, during Salome's Dance of the Seven Veils, I was in a dungeon below stage and through the grate I could gaze up at Margot's half naked body writhing erotically just inches from my face. It was almost more than I could endure, and from that time onward

I always thought of her as "Margo, the Body!" She appeared in many of Richard's adaptations of *Amphitryon* and *Undine*, and in later years also moved on to Hollywood.

In those early years, the Players produced a new play each week, with performances on Thursday, Friday, and Saturday nights. In the event of rain, a performance would be re-scheduled to Sunday night. The logistics of this meant that at the beginning of each week we'd be madly scrambling to memorize our lines, help build scenery and rehearse the new production. Frequently, we did not have time to really develop our roles nor truly inhabit the character, although usually by Saturday night we were fairly proficient. Rehearsals often ran late into the night, and the pace was so stressful that at times you prayed to be cast in just a minor role like a maid or butler, which did not require many lines to memorize.

In those early years the theatre had no roof over the audience. I remember one opening night when there was a fierce wind blowing across the bay and it was all we could do to project our voices past the stage—we were literally shouting to be heard. The following night, the show was cancelled due to gale force winds and drenching rain, but by Sunday the skies had cleared long enough for the play to be performed. It was not until 1946 that finally a huge canvas top, designed by local shipbuilders and riggers, protected the audience from the weather. But this too proved to be unsatisfactory because in strong winds the canvas would flap loudly unless 12 or more people clung desperately to its lower edges. It also tended to bulge with rainwater during storms, and at regular intervals had to be poked at with long poles, often drenching the patrons in the process.

During that first season Caroline claimed to have about 200 regular subscribers. I remember accompanying her on a drive along Cottage Row in Fish Creek where the millionaires from Chicago, St. Louis and Milwaukee had summer homes. I suppose I looked like a presentable young actor and we sold four subscriptions that morning. Of course, the ticket price was about a dollar so a subscription could only have been $10 or so. Another jaunt with Caroline was a drive to Ellison Bay to visit Jens Jensen who had some interesting Scandinavian furniture that she hoped to borrow for one of the productions. Mr. Jensen was the noted landscape architect who designed Grant Park and Garfield Park in Chicago, and later his home in Ellison Bay became "The Clearing." On the way we stopped for coffee at Al Johnson's in Sister Bay, which at that time was just a tiny white cottage on the bay. Caroline knew everyone in Door County. She was a one-woman public relations machine and would regularly canvas the county with playbills to promote each production.

To celebrate the opening of the first play of the season there was usually a reception held in the middle of July, which guaranteed a good-sized crowd for that evening's performance. It was such a gala affair that it actually made headlines in the society page of the *Chicago Tribune,* where it was described as the "leading event of the week in Door County," so you can see that, indeed, the Players lent an air of elegance and distinction to the area. We were always pleased when we'd have an audience of about 150 people, and on rare nights 260 people would constitute a sell-out, standing room only crowd. Audiences of this size flocked to the 1938 performances of *Night Must Fall,* the Emlyn Williams thriller. It starred Leo Lucker, the Player's consummate actor and director, in the role of the seemingly innocent and kindly Welsh murderer. In fact, in all my 65 years in the theatre, I have never seen anyone play the part as well as Leo. Leo, along with Richard Fisher, was the Player's resident director for the next twenty years, and during that period he also played in many important roles on the New York stage.

One of the memorable character actresses in those early years was a Miss Gertrude Needham, a British actress who somehow strayed into the Midwest, ran out of work, and then was stranded there. Caroline or Richard had met her in

Chicago, introduced her to Mama, and I think she then moved in with the Fishers. Richard absolutely adored her because she knew so much about theatre. Besides playing leading character roles, she also taught diction to the young apprentices and acted as a kind of chaperone.

Another person who played an important role in the success of the fledgling company was the actress, Helen "Casey" Bragdon, who was associated with the Players from its inception until 1958. She was a Smith College graduate and a method actress who had studied with the Russians, Andrius Jelinsky and Madame Soloviova, and had previously acted in summer stock out East. I always felt she had been born old; she had an aura of seriousness and reserve about her. She functioned as Caroline's assistant, assuming much of the administrative work of the theatre, which she performed in an efficient and organized manner; she was extremely modest about her accomplishments, however, never taking any credit for herself. She was also a very gifted and elegant character actress, appearing in many roles at the Players. Eventually she moved on to the Flatrock Summer Theatre in North Carolina where she remained for many years.

Caroline returned from Hollywood rather suddenly in July of 1938; it was announced that she would be arriving in a few minutes and everyone should immediately drop whatever they were doing (we were in the midst of dress rehearsal for a play which was opening the following evening!) and walk up the hill as a group to greet Caroline and her friend Julie Bishop, another Hollywood starlet, when they stepped off the Bayview bus. A tremendous fuss was made as if it was royalty who were about to appear! Of course, the thought of Hollywood was like a Shangri-la to us Midwesterners. For all we knew, it was on the other side of the world! During my years at the Goodman, Hollywood agents did visit the school from time to time, but I could never picture myself in the movies because I wasn't handsome enough. Even as a young actor I was always playing old men, never the romantic lead or the lover.

At some time during Caroline's year in Hollywood she had met Rodion Rathbone, son of the well-known British actor, Basil Rathbone, of Sherlock Holmes fame, and by the end of 1938 they were married. Rodion looked nothing like his father, but was just a tall, skinny round-faced kid, about 22 years old at the time, with a British accent. I found him to be very open and friendly. He didn't care to be an actor like his father but had an engineering degree from England, and now worked as a navigator for TWA. During that summer of 1939 he visited the Players occasionally, and I remember sitting with him in the lodge that September listening to the radio and hearing that Hitler had just invaded Poland. This was terribly disturbing to him because it meant that war in Europe was imminent, and he would have to join the Royal Canadian Air Force.

In my final year at the Goodman I had an apartment on Ohio and Michigan, just around the corner from Caroline and Rodion, who lived near Huron. At the time, they were still newlyweds and deeply in love; however, their temperaments were highly volatile, and occasionally during a heated argument they'd end up throwing things at each other. Every once in a while I'd get a hysterical call from Caroline—it could be two in the morning—and she'd say, "Bob, you've got to come over and try to make Rodion happy!" I would walk over to their apartment, and I'd start by mincing around, waving my wrists, and saying "Rodion honey…you sweet thing…you dear boy…" (During summers at the Players, Rodion and I used to play at being fags, we had a complete routine worked out.) And as soon as he heard these words, he'd scream, "Thstop it, thstopit!" each word delivered in a swishy lisp. And then I'd scold him, saying, "Rodion honey, why are you doing this to Caroline?" Before long we'd all be laughing hysterically, Rodion and Caroline would be happy, and I could go back home to bed again!

A cherished tradition which occurred every Labor Day, at the end of the Players summer season, was a visit from Eva Klingbile, a large impressive woman who was the unofficial mayor of Juddville and owner of the general store and gas station on Highway 42 and Juddville Road, where many of the Players bought snacks or cigarettes. She brought sandwiches and several bottles of her homemade cherry and dandelion wines which were practically lethal in their potency and we all sat around together celebrating the end of another season. She died some years ago and there is a memorial stone for her in the garden south of the theatre that reads simply, "Eva's Garden".

When I finally graduated from the Goodman in June 1940, I determined that as much as I loved the Peninsula Players, I was never going to be discovered or become famous as long as I remained in this bucolic theatre tucked away in the backwoods of Wisconsin. I decided that it was time for me to try my luck in the bright city lights of New York!

Chapter 6
Broadway Here I Come!

Like countless young actors before me, I went to New York in June 1940 with the highest of hopes. After all, I had letters of introduction to Leland Hayward, New York's most important theatrical agent, from Basil Rathbone's son Rodion, and also from the son of that other famous Shakespearean actor, Philip Merivale. In addition, Mary Agnes Doyle, my beloved diction teacher from the Goodman, had penned several letters to her New York theatre friends extolling my virtues as an actor. As for a place to stay, two maiden cousins of my mother, Misses Letty Layton and Edna Randall who lived just across from Manhattan in Maplewood, New Jersey, had offered me temporary lodgings.

I remember visiting Mr. Hayward's office where I was received very cordially. I showed him my certificate from the Goodman, my letters of introduction, and also some small 3x5 photographs of character roles I had played. He was extremely friendly and as I sat there I thought to myself, "I'm almost on my way to success right now!" Glancing around the room, I noticed a huge photograph of Tyrone Powers that completely filled up one wall, while countless other stars beamed down at me from around the room. Mr. Hayward finally said to me, "I'm sorry Mr. Thompson. I really can't do anything for you until I see you in a show, so what I suggest you do is get into a show…and once you're in a show, be sure to let me know and I'll come to see you." Immediately I realized the Catch 22 of my situation: I couldn't get into a show unless an agent recommended me, and I couldn't get an agent to recommend me until they had seen me in a show. Once out on the pavement again, I tore up my worthless recommendations and tossed them into the nearest trash can!

I had given myself one year to succeed in New York and I certainly wasn't going to call it quits now. I had traveled from Chicago by bus so I had no transportation. I bought myself a car for $35; it was a 1931 Model A Ford one- seater with a rumble seat. It ran O.K. but I had to spend $100 more in improvements to bring it up to standard in order to pass the New Jersey vehicle inspection. I had brought with me a list of all the East Coast playhouses that I had written to in previous years and I was determined to stop at every one of them until I found work.

Saying goodbye to my maiden aunts in Maplewood, New Jersey, I tossed my suitcase into the rumble seat and set off on a rainy Friday morning in June. I drove across the George Washington Bridge through upper Manhattan and headed for the Connecticut shore. My first stop was the Stamford Theatre where I presented my credentials to Nat Burns, the grandnephew or grandson of Nat C. Goodwin, a famous actor from the turn of the century. Although he was in the midst of a rehearsal, he stopped to talk to me for twenty minutes or so. He was quite friendly and I remember that the whole cast gathered around us to listen too. I became the center of attention because they were amazed that an unknown actor who doesn't have an agent would just appear unannounced looking for work. Nat Burns was very encouraging and said that if he had had a spot for me, he would have hired me. I thanked him for his time, then asked him where was the next closest theatre. He said, "Westport Playhouse" and gave me directions there. My last glimpse, as I drove off and honked, was the entire cast waving to me.

The next stop was the Westport Playhouse, which I later learned was the summer stock theatre for the Theatre Guild associated with the well-known director Guthrie McClintic, husband of Katherine Cornell. I received a rather chilly reception there which consisted of, "Why are you stopping here...we don't hire anyone unless they are already members of the Theatre Guild!" I inquired where the next theatre was, and they directed me to the Plymouth Playhouse which was about two hours away.

I arrived in Milford, Connecticut by mid-afternoon. It was a typical charming New England town and the Playhouse was located in the eighteenth century townhall on the square. The girl at the box office was rather friendly and I soon learned that she was Priscilla Jameson, wife of the leading actor. I explained to her that I was from Chicago, I had no agent, and here were my credentials from the Goodman Theatre. She told me later that she was so intrigued by this rather earnest and personable young man who materialized out of nowhere without even some decent 8x10 photographs that she decided to offer me something. "Have you done any backstage work?" she asked, and I told her that as part of my four year Goodman scholarship I was required to assist with all the evening productions, so I was proficient in working the lightboard, working the moving scenery and the stage curtains. She explained to me that the following weekend they were doing the play *Margin for Error* by Clare Booth Luce, and Otto Preminger was coming to play the lead role. However, they hadn't cast his secretary yet but I was about the right age, so she offered the part to me. Then I asked her where I would live, and she said there was a rooming house run by an English lady just off the square. She then introduced me to Frank Gaunt, the producing director of the Playhouse, who also mentioned that they were expecting Otto Preminger to arrive any day now. I drove over to the rooming house where I remarked to the landlady that my grandfather, Edward Mealing Thompson, was also from England. She showed me to my room and said she'd fix me a meal shortly. I was absolutely in heaven! I'd found a job, a place to stay, I was going to be fed—I had everything I wanted. Within five hours of leaving New York, I had found a place to land!

The next morning was Saturday and I was given a copy of the script. In reading the play, I realized that the role of the German Consul, an arrogant Nazi to be played by Otto Preminger, was a very powerful part. Saturday went by and still no word from Preminger. That night I decided to study the part. I knew what a German should sound like; I could do the accent. So I decided that if Preminger didn't come, I would try out for his role. All day Sunday I practiced the part of the German Consul in my room. He gets murdered in the first act anyway, and I figured I could manage to sustain the role that long. Monday morning arrives and still no word from Preminger. At that point the director Frank Gaunt was considering the possibility of contacting a German professor at Yale to do the part. I continued to study the role in my room. Finally the Playhouse called Otto Preminger and was told that for some reason he couldn't come. They were all stunned by this news, and I remember Gaunt sitting with some of the actors and the tech crew on the wide front steps of the Playhouse, wondering what to do next. I came out and told them that I would like to read for the part of the German Consul. I had memorized it by now so I asked them to cue me. When I had finished they said, "My God, you sound just like the Consul, but can you play a 45 year old?" I assured them I could and was given the part. I had the next four or five days to rehearse before the play opened. All I had to do was sustain the character through the first act, and then the Consul is murdered. The play was performed that weekend as planned and the reviews from the *Bridgeport Post*, July 23, 1940, stated:

> *"Special honors go to Robert Thompson for his excellent portrayal of the German Consul, an arrogant domineering, brutal sadist, who typifies all that is detested in the Nazi regime and gives no fewer than seven people adequate reason for wanting to kill him. They do, in fact, all attempt it and actually poison, stab, and shoot him but when the mystery of his death is unraveled in the second act, he is found to have cheated them by taking his own life.*

Mr. Thompson, a newcomer to the Milford Company, is a versatile actor with extensive stock and radio experience who was brought here by Frank Gaunt, the director, especially for the part. His performance raised the level of the entire production."

Of course, I was extremely gratified by the positive review, and my stock within the company itself rose sky high. However, I also was shocked to discover the first canon of theatre promotion which is *to exaggerate, to hype, and, if necessary, stretch the truth!* The fact that I was a callow, unemployed actor who had just materialized out of nowhere in an old jalopy one week previously didn't seem to enter into the equation. By the end of that summer, my performance as Karl Baumer, the German Consul, had been rated one of the ten best performances in all stock playhouses on the East Coast!

I settled in very comfortably at the Plymouth Playhouse for the rest of the season and was given many of the lead roles. The next play was *Our Town* by Thornton Wilder. The previous year at the Goodman I had played the lead as the Stage Manager who narrates the play. However, as this part was already cast, I played Dr. Gibbs, an old man, instead. The third play of the season was Clare Boothe Luce's satire *Kiss the Boys Goodbye* where I finally played a younger man, the movie magnate Herbert Z. Harner. The Bridgeport Post, August 13, 1940, commented:

"Robert Thompson finally has a role which comes close to revealing his true age (only 23). As a German Consul in Margin for Error, *he did a splendid job, but the audience hated him! As Dr. Gibbs in* Our Town *he was old again. Now as the great Hollywood director he still appears older than he is, but no less handsome. Now he is setting Milford female hearts fluttering. But the girls should see him offstage and hear his rich voice...."*

(All music to my ears, although I can't say that the Milford girls were beating a path to my door!)

Kiss The Boys Goodbye was held over for a week because of excellent box office sales. In the meantime, we were simultaneously rehearsing for the next show, *Cat and the Canary*, which they had asked me to direct. It was now the third week in August and we had very good audiences because most of the neighboring playhouses were closing down for the season. The final play was *No Time for Comedy*, which was performed over the Labor Day weekend, and then we too ended our season.

I was convinced that it was only a matter of time before I'd become a success on Broadway because I did so well at the Plymouth Playhouse. In September Frank Gaunt and I decided to room together in Manhattan. We moved into the St. James, a hotel for unemployed actors at 45th and Times Square. Our rent was $15 a week, we had a hot plate to cook on, and in the winter we kept food in a box out on the windowsill. While looking for work at NBC studios, I had run into my old friend from the Goodman, Buddy Berens, who had just come to New York, so he became our third roommate. Buddy was also a dancer and had taught me the "time step" so I could accompany him on cattle calls at the theatres.

Frank Gaunt was slightly older than me, a debonaire fellow who resembled a pipe-smoking Gregory Peck. What I didn't realize was that he was also a gambler and played the horses. He spent much of the time at the racetrack and was always cadging money from me. "Just let me have $5 more, I'll pay you back when my trust money comes in." Apparently he had some rich father or grandfather so he could be feckless about his finances. Eventually I lost $50 to him, but the unpleasant experience taught me an important lesson in life. Never loan someone money until you've at least been paid back for the initial sum.

The St. James was a family run hotel and the owners were kind to actors. We had a telephone in our room in case theatres or agents needed to contact us. There was a dining room, a lobby, and a public typewriter. I immediately got a job as a busboy at Toffinetti's Restaurant where I was paid 20 cents an hour plus tips and one free meal. I worked the evening shift from 5 to 9 so it didn't interfere with my looking for theatre work. I worked there only a few weeks because I soon learned that the waitresses were reluctant to share their tips with us and were quite vicious in their dislike of chintzy customers who left only a meager gratuity.

My life consisted of making the daily rounds of the casting offices and theatres where you were persona non grata—nobody wanted you. You never got past the agent or producer's front office, which was always guarded by an indifferent secretary who usually said, "Nothing for you today!!" I eventually developed a little routine to protect my ego from the unrelenting rejection. I would breeze into the front office and in a nonchalant voice say, "I know you don't have anything for me today, but I'd just like to hear you tell me that!" This usually made the secretary laugh, and it somehow made me feel better too. During this time I was constantly following up on potential leads from any connections that I had from the Plymouth Playhouse. As a result, I had received a letter from the Mercury Theatre, founded in 1937 by Orson Welles; they were casting the play *Woodrow Wilson*. I read for the part along with four other actors, but was not called back for a second reading.

In October I started working as an usher at the Rivoli Theatre on Times Square for $15 a week. My attire was a dove-gray morning coat with razor-crease pinstriped trousers, gaiters and gloves. It was quite an elegant movie theatre where I was able to see all the first run movies. A good Chinese dinner in those days cost only 25 cents, so financially I was doing all right. My living expenses were $5 for my share of the hotel room, $5 per week for food and $5 saved for a rainy day—I was doing O.K.!

My mother visited me sometime in October. I think she thought I needed some encouragement. Meanwhile, because of the war in Europe, I had to register for the draft. I applied at NBC for work as a page in the guest relations staff; and after the interview, I was riding down in the elevator when a formally dressed gentleman with hat and cane got in. It was Arturo Toscanini who, at that time, was the conductor of the NBC Symphony! I just had to talk to him, so I stuck out my hand and smiled, "Hello, I'm Robert Thompson from Chicago." He glanced over at me and said "Uh?" End of our conversation. I felt terribly embarrassed and thought what a jackass thing to do. His thoughts were probably completely immersed in music, and perhaps he only conversed in Italian. *Nevertheless, I had talked with Arturo Toscanini!!*

I joined a young people's group at St. Nicholas Dutch Reformed Church on 48th Street and Fifth Avenue where I made some new friends. As it turned out, they were planning to put on a play, a comedy called *The Patsy,* and they asked me to direct it. Because I was still employed as an usher, I had to fit rehearsal time in after work, which made for late nights.

By mid-November I was feeling pretty bleak and disillusioned. It had been raining for 3 days straight, and my good friend and fellow roommate, Buddy Berens, had decided to go back home. He had run out of money, was returning to Madison, Wisconsin, to work in his uncle's gas station, and was taking his radio with him. The hotel room was pretty dismal now, quiet and depressing, as was the whole atmosphere of the St. James with so many actors out of work, and especially older actors who at one time had been at the top of their field, and now were practically begging producers for work. It was so demeaning to witness, so demoralizing.

I spent Thanksgiving with the maiden aunts in Maplewood, New Jersey. My ushering job ended, so I applied for a job at Macy's during the Christmas season and was hired as a demonstrator in the Children's Toyland Department for $18 a week plus commission and an evening meal. The job was a pretext so I could tell my mother that I was unable to come home for Christmas because I knew in my heart that if I went home, I would never return to New York. It was too discouraging, too emotionally bleak for me.

During the Christmas season Macy's Toyland was an anthill of little brats squirming around the aisles grabbing anything they could possibly get their hands on. My job was to demonstrate a toy called the "Ro-Blo" which was similar to a child's peddle-car but was built with the restrictions of apartment living in mind. When seated on the "Ro-Blo" the child would begin to row like the Furies were after him, and the resulting motion inflated a rubber balloon, which then sailed into the air with a tremendous "whoosh"! The devoted parent could place this contraption either in the living room or even out on a balcony where their little angel would have fresh air, yet be in no danger of being hit by a car or snatched by a kidnapper; and all the while their arm, leg, shoulder, back and stomach muscles were receiving a sound work-out. (The toy would also presumably tire them out sufficiently so that later they would take a nap!) When I demonstrated the "Ro-Blo", usually a crowd gathered around to listen to my spiel. (A ham actor can create quite a diversion!) However, when my performance was done I usually sold only one or two, although occasionally someone would come up to me and say, "Please send three of them to this address!"

My former English landlady invited me to spend the holidays in Milford, Connecticut, where a snowstorm on Christmas Eve transformed the town square into a Currier and Ives postcard. We climbed over snowdrifts to reach the Presbyterian Church whose festive interior was decorated with evergreen boughs, red poinsettias and glowing candlelight. I remember listening to glorious Christmas music with some of my friends from the Playhouse, but I missed my family back in Illinois.

During this time I was working with a small theatre group that performed plays off-Broadway. One of the plays was *The Perfect Understanding* by Ivan Sokoloff at the Cherry

Lane Theatre in Greenwich Village. This was always unpaid work; you were just hoping the critics would come to the play and write a good review. In addition I occasionally did some radio work at NBC, also unpaid.

In February I auditioned for and was given the lead in a Noel Coward Play, *Post Mortem*, an anti-war play inspired by the horrors of World War I. The production was being mounted by the Hilltop Theatre group who, during the winter season, performed in a theatre-in-the-round in Greenwich Village. At the same time, I was ushering again eight hours a day in a frock coat, black cravat, spats and white gloves, this time at the Hollywood movie theatre, while rehearsing the play in the evening. The performance played to good houses during its March run and was generally well received. As a result, I was invited to join the Hilltop Theatre group, which during the 13 week summer season performed at Ellicott City, Maryland just outside Baltimore. Around Easter time I had visited the local draft board in New York where I learned that my number was 2611, which meant I might be drafted by summertime. I was hoping for the best because I was really looking forward to playing good parts with this Equity company.

The Hilltop Theatre was housed in an imposing 1838 mansion on a ten- acre estate complete with swimming pool, and overlooking the rolling hills of the Patapsco River Valley. Just one hour from Washington DC, New York theatrical agents occasionally visited looking for new talent. The vista from my second floor window was an impressive sweep across the river valley to the mountain range beyond. I had arrived in May to help clean up the place and paint some of the rooms. The theatre was owned by the Don Swann family and there were about 36 in the company. I was chosen to play the lead in the first show, *Love From a Stranger* by Frank Vospar. It was directed by Wendell K. Phillips, who had also been at the Goodman, and knew Dr. Gnesin, Doyle and Itken; I felt that I was in familiar company. After opening night there was a cast party where Dick Angarola and I entertained, he on cello and me playing the guitar. (Dick was a few years behind me at the Goodman, and he played at the Peninsula Players during the 1940 and 1945 summer seasons.)

I met a beautiful girl at the Hilltop, a young actress named Natalie Chilvers whose nickname was "Chat". She lived in Manhattan, and her Jewish mother was a wonderful cook who comforted me with chicken soup if I was coming down with bronchitis or some other ailment. I thought Chat and I might form an acting duo like Lunt and Fontanne and we played together that summer in *Private Lives* by Noel Coward. The lead was played by a well-known actress, Margaret Barker, who was drunk much of the time and ad-libbed her way through many of the scenes. It was very disconcerting for the rest of us, although the critics didn't seem to notice and called her work "brilliant and sophisticated."

The balance of the Hilltop season was *The Divorcons* by Margaret Mayo, *The Gorilla* by Ralph Spence, and a Labor Day finale, *All Done with Mirrors* by Green and Dibble. All of the plays were previewed first at nearby Fort Meade for the benefit of the troops. This is when I began to have misgivings about the wisdom of joining the Army infantry. Most of the guys didn't give a fig about the play; all they wanted to do was hoot and holler the minute a female set foot on stage.

At the very end of the Hilltop season I was finally discovered by the theatre agent, Eve Gincher, or should I say, "rediscovered." It happened this way. The previous year I had visited her office in the Sardi Building. She was engaged on the telephone, and I overheard her say that a 24 year-old character actor was needed for a particular part. Immediately I said to her, "I could do that…send me!" Putting her hand over the receiver, she hissed at me, "But I don't even know you!" As I left her office I vowed that I'd never deal with her again. But now a year had past, she and her brother had seen one of my performances at the Hilltop, and they had come backstage afterwards. "You were simply marvelous, Mr. Thompson," she gushed, "but haven't we met somewhere before?" I bit my tongue and lied saying, "I don't believe so," but I felt like telling her, "Yes, I'm the poor sod you wouldn't give the time of day to when I visited your office a year ago!" However, sometime later she wrote me a wonderful letter of introduction to Lee Strasberg who was casting *Clash by Night*, which would star Tallulah Bankhead:

Dear Mr. Strasberg,

This is Robert Thompson who was so excellent this summer in stock. I hope you will give him a reading for "Joe" as I feel he is really one of the most promising boys this season. Thank you.

Eve

To audition for the part of Joe, I went to Billy Rose's apartment in Manhattan where I read before the playwright, Clifford Odets, and Strasberg himself. They both liked my reading but, in the end, remarked, "We can't hire you, Mr. Thompson, because you have no name recognition on Broadway at all…you are an unknown. We have to hire someone with a name!" Eventually, they gave the part to Robert Ryan, and Lee J. Cobb starred opposite Tallulah who was temperamental throughout the play's run, and fought constantly with the producer, Billy Rose, and the rest of the cast.

In the middle of September, I received my draft notice. I was classified as 1-A and was invited to report for induction at Fort Dix, New Jersey, on October 7, 1941. My theatre career in New York was over, for the time being at least.

Chapter 7
The War Years 1941-46

I had vowed I would never return to New York again to look for work in the theatre. I had begun to hate the anonymity of the city where no one knew you, and no one cared about you. The only way I would ever come back to that city is if I already had a job to come to, or that I was somehow already in a play which moved on to Broadway—those would be my only terms. So, in a way, being drafted had given me a legitimate excuse to leave the city, the city that had no use for my theatre craft. Now I had been asked to serve my country and I went into the Army with the attitude that I didn't want to tell anyone that I was an actor; I didn't want to put any emphasis on it at all. Instead, I would do anything the Army wanted me to do.

I reported to Fort Dix, New Jersey, on October 7, 1941. A few days later a representative from the Army Air Corps came to speak to the inductees and explained that if we enlisted in the Air Corps for three years, we would not only get a $9 a month pay raise but we could also move from a tent to the barracks, and would have the opportunity to go to school. Of course, with my Boy Scout background I had an affinity for tenting in the rough. All the same, the prospect of a solid roof over my head with no rain seeping through the canvas, plus an extra $9 a month, sounded like a good deal to me! Two days later I enlisted in the Air Corps and immediately went to the barracks and $30 monthly pay. They asked me where I wanted to go to school. My choices were: Hickham Field, Hawaii; Scott Field in Illinois; Madison, Wisconsin; or somewhere in South Dakota, and then I had a further choice of either radio communications or gunnery school. Well, of course, gunnery school was where they taught you all about guns and munitions which I wanted no part of, whereas I already had radio experience. Without hesitation, I chose radio communications and Scott Field in Belleville, Illinois, which was relatively close to home. Homesickness, I suppose, also played a part, because I had been in New York for almost a year and a half, and Belleville was not far from Springfield, Illinois, where my beloved Aunt Faye was now working. At this time, my mother's health was not too good so I would have more of a chance to see her.

While at basic training at Fort Dix, New Jersey, I visited New York one last time. My old friend, Sam Wanamaker from the Goodman, had become rather important in radio broadcasting and now had a big office at RCA in Rockefeller Center. (Sam acted at the Peninsula Players in 1937 and went on to become an important Hollywood movie producer, and was instrumental in the recreation of Shakespeare's Globe Theatre on the Thames.) It was no problem getting in to see him, but instead of the friendly reception I had anticipated, he was rather curt and formal and it only gradually dawned on me that he assumed I had come to ask him for a job, despite the fact I was in uniform and already had a job with the U.S. Army! It was a real shock for me and I thought if this is what success can do to you, make you forget old friends, then this was not the success I desired. I had come really to reminisce about the good old days at the Goodman, but I left his office with the feeling I didn't want to see him again.

At Scott Air Force Base in Belleville, Illinois I studied radio communication, learning about transmitters, receivers and Morse code. On our day off many of the guys would head for the bars and dance halls in nearby St. Louis where, in the wee hours, they'd end up involved in "hanky panky!" But if you were a Boy Scout *and* a Methodist like I was, you went to the USO which hosted dances with respectable girls, Cokes and homemade cookies! Through the USO I met the Lodwick family who had 3 or 4 daughters who regularly attended the dances. Mrs. Lodwick sort of adopted me and I was welcome at their home every Monday, my day off. I never dated any of the sisters, they treated me more like a brother, but occasionally they arranged dates for me with their girlfriends. Mrs. Lodwick was a wonderful cook, so for me the Lodwicks represented "home" as my own home was 300 miles away. I sometimes helped Mrs. Lodwick with the laundry, and I was free to read or study or do whatever I wanted to do while visiting there.

On the morning of December 7, 1941, we had just turned on the radio when our squadron heard the news that Pearl Harbor had been bombed by the Japanese. That was the end of all normal life as we knew it. All Christmas leaves were cancelled. I also realized that had I chosen Hickham Field, Hawaii, as my first posting, I might have been killed at Pearl Harbor.

I remained at Scott Field for two years as a radio communications instructor, during which time I advanced from Private to Private First Class to Corporal to Sergeant, all the while teaching kids who were eventually assigned to be radio operators on the B-17 (the Flying Fortress) and B-24 bombers. However, after a while, I realized I would be stuck at Scott Field until the end of the war, so I decided to apply for Cadet School (officers training school). I was accepted, became a Cadet, and was sent to Boca Raton, Florida for ten weeks of officers training at the Boca Raton Club, the one time haunt of the gangster Al Capone. It was an elegant, five-story building with palm trees, golf course and swimming pool, but by the time I got there the golf course had been converted to a parade ground. Our next posting was a six-week stint at Yale University for completion of officers training. There we were entertained by the Glenn Miller Orchestra in the mess hall, and presumably the elevated ambiance of those Gothic quadrangles helped transform us into officers and gentlemen.

It was now September 1943, I was 27 years old, and my next assignment was Tomah, Wisconsin, where I would attend the early radar, or control net system. First I visited my mother in Downers Grove. I was in uniform and when she greeted me at the door her first words were, "Rob, you've lost a lot of weight, are you O.K.? Are you feeling all right?" But the truth was my mother was not well and had just a few more weeks to live. She entered the hospital with terminal cancer, and during the next six weeks I came home every weekend to visit her.

During these home visits my sister Eleanor, who had been caring for my mother, and the neighbors, decided I needed a girlfriend, so they fixed me up with a girl from La Grange named Sally Kolk. After visiting my mother at the hospital, I would take Sally out on a date, usually to some nice restaurant like the Yar or other fancy places on Randolph Street. Once I asked her to come canoeing with me, so we drove to the Fox River at St. Charles where my canoe "The Driftwood" was stored. However, she didn't much like canoeing and, in fact, she wasn't interested in doing any of that normal kind of stuff...the things that I enjoyed like camping or canoeing. All she really liked to do was to be taken to fancy restaurants, expensive restaurants that cost a lot of dough.

My mother died on November 4, 1943, at age 65, and I was very much affected by her death. She had been the emotional heart of our family, with her abundant love and concern, her many letters of encouragement to me in New York and in the service, and now she was gone. During those weeks she was hospitalized I knew she was dying yet there was such a feeling of unreality, and now the shock—the finality of it all. I took it very hard. I had to make the funeral arrangements and purchase the burial plots at Clarendon Hills Cemetery. For some reason my father was unable to do it.

In the emotional aftermath of the funeral my neighbors suggested that I should consider getting engaged to Sally

Kolk. After all, I was going off to war, my mother was dead, and I needed someone who would write to me. During wartime there were many hasty engagements and marriages when the possibility of death was very real and life could be brief. I was tempted by their advice so I bought her a ring. I told her I didn't know where I was going to be posted or when I was coming back. But the minute I returned to the base, I knew I had made a terrible mistake! I knew this was for the birds, it wasn't for me at all! We had nothing in common! First of all, she didn't like canoeing or the outdoor life—all she wanted was someone who would take her to fancy places. I knew I had to write her and gradually, over a period of time, tell her that I was having second thoughts. I would suggest that we cancel the engagement, and if she wanted to send back the ring to me, that would be fine. I knew this relationship would never work.

I was transferred to Bradley Field in Windsor Locks, Connecticut, while awaiting reassignment. I went skiing in the Berkshires with my friend, Harold Phillippo, and we also put on a musical called "The Battle of Bradley" which we eventually took to the Stage Door Canteen in New York. Every winter while at the Goodman I had had a problem with sore throats, and Bradley Field was no different. One of the base doctors suggested I have my tonsils out—the recovery period would be no problem, perhaps five days in the hospital. I decided to have it done and while I was in the hospital recuperating, the rest of my squadron received orders to leave immediately for the South Pacific where they would serve as radar technicians. Over half of those men never came home again!

I was transferred to Lowry Field in Denver, Colorado, where I attended school nine hours a day for the next ten weeks. I was assigned to central fire control on the B-29 bomber, a new plane just developed by Boeing. When the course was finished I was sent to the Boeing plant in Oklahoma City where there was a huge mock-up of the B-

29, an *enormous* plane! I was the officer in charge of the electrical firing systems. I was no mechanical wizard but somehow I had to learn this whole gigantic system. By contrast, my father was an electrical genius who could figure out a schematic in an instant, yet in practical matters he could barely change a light bulb—that had been my mother's bailiwick. When I was at the Boeing school, my father came to visit me and we took a drive to Tucumcari, New Mexico, where he was supervising some electrical power installation. In light of my brief engagement the previous year, I remember asking him, "How do you know when you're in love, Dad...how can you tell when it's the real thing?" He was clearly embarrassed by this personal talk and muttered, "That's rubbish, you'll know when it happens, you'll know when you find it!" or words to that effect. Well, this didn't help me at all because I didn't know what the answer was, and I was trying to get from this intelligent man a good straight answer, but most of the time he never gave me any direct answers. We never really understood each other.

In 1944 I became a First Lieutenant and joined the 25th Air Depot group, which was responsible for the maintenance of the B-29 bombers. We were transferred to Fort Lawton in Seattle awaiting transport to the South Pacific. As a diversion a buddy and I rented a small boat to go salmon fishing for a few days, but we never caught anything. One day we noticed a young kid who had a whole boat filled with huge salmon he had caught. We bought one for $3 and took it back to the base claiming we had bagged it. We put it on ice in the refrigerator, but the order to board ship for Hawaii came so quickly that, in the confusion, we left our prize salmon behind. We had been savouring the taste of that fish, and during the 6-day voyage we often lamented its loss. Our ship anchored in Pearl Harbor where the bombed out metal hulks of the fleet were everywhere to be seen. We were awaiting an escort convoy but we weren't told our final destination. Guam was 10 days away, and during the voyage the card sharks and gamblers ruled the decks. Fortunately, I had had that earlier experience with my gambling roommate, Frank Gaunt, so I was not tempted to join in—I knew nothing about poker anyway. Cigarettes were 50 cents a carton in 1944 and I had learned to smoke at the Goodman in order to play the sophisticate in Noel Coward plays, so this was my only vice.

We landed in Guam, which had been secured, but there were still Japanese hiding in jungle caves and tunnels who hadn't surrendered yet. We were not allowed to carry guns, however, because the commanders were afraid we'd shoot at any suspicious rustling noises in the bush and end up killing each other. During my year in Guam I was in charge of maintaining the generators that supplied the electricity to the mess halls and to various squadrons. We slept in tents where we were plagued with overwhelming heat and humidity that burst into afternoon downpours. The rank jungle, waiting just beyond the airfield's perimeter, was rife with pockmarked shell holes. On base was a large casualty hospital where the maimed and wounded were gathered from various hotspots in the Pacific theatre.

About two weeks after the Battle of Iwo Jima, a friend asked me if I'd like to fly with him to see the island. We boarded the plane, and as it raced down the runway the pilot and co-pilot were arguing about the takeoff speed. One was screaming, "You've got to go faster...*go faster*!!" And meanwhile the jungle at the end of the runway was looming closer and closer, and at the very last second we pulled up, barely skimming the treetops. Not an auspicious start!

Once we landed at Iwo Jima we took a walk through the shattered jungle where wisps of sulphur were rising from the battleground and skirting around shell holes we glimpsed human body parts scattered here and there. With the humidity and heat, the stench was overwhelming—it was literally Hell on Earth! All I could think was that the soldiers who had survived this battle were undoubtedly scarred for life by the experience. There were no real winners in this game of death!

I survived the war only through some hand of fate. I could have been killed at Pearl Harbor in December 1941 if I had chosen the tropical lure of Hawaii as my first assignment. If I had not had my tonsils out in late 1943 I would have been shipped out with the rest of my squadron to the Pacific where over half the men were killed. My childhood friend from Garfield Park, Carl Lervold, was killed, as was Buddy Berens, my Manhattan roommate who taught me how to tap dance.

During the 15 day sea voyage back from the Pacific I had many nights to reflect on my experience, and I'd look up at the stars and pray, "Dear God, if you have any influence, what I'd like to do is teach theatre at a college because theatre is all I know." I didn't have the slightest idea what I was going to do once I got out of the service. All I wanted was the sane and predictable world of a college campus with honest, normal people.

Chapter 8
Rosary College

While I was in Guam, my sister Eleanor had sent me a photograph of a very pretty girl sitting on my beloved canoe, "Driftwood", and so began a year-long correspondence with Miss Margaret Porter. She was a music teacher in the Downers Grove schools and my sister's best friend. During that year we learned everything about each other—our values, our goals, and our dreams. We both shared a love of music, theatre, travel, adventure and, besides being a Methodist, Margaret also loved the out-doors, camping and canoeing! *This was an ideal girl!* She was talented and smart with a master's degree in music from Northwestern; and all that remained, once we finally met in person, was to see if we really liked each other. When I stepped off the train in Downers Grove on January 3, 1946, my father, my sister, and Miss Porter were waiting for me on the platform. I looked at Miss Porter: she had two eyes, two ears, and her nose was in the right place, so I thought, "O.K. this is good." Actually, I thought she looked *wonderful*!!!!

Two weeks after my return to Chicago, and while still in uniform, I went to see my former teachers at the Goodman, Dr. Gnesin, Mary Agnes Doyle, and David B. Itken, to ask their advice about securing a job to teach theatre. It was just a few days later when I received a call from Miss Doyle who said, "Robert, I want you to see Sister Mary Peter, the President of Rosary College. They are looking for a person to teach theatre for one semester." (The previous instructor had left for a better position).

Rosary College was a highly respected Catholic girls school in River Forest, a wealthy Chicago suburb. My interview was with Sister Mary Gregory, the head of the theatre department with an MA degree in theatre from the University of Iowa. "Sister Greg" was a youngish woman who seemed to be teasing me during the interview because she was aware I was dying for a cigarette, but was too embarrassed to ask her permission to smoke. At the time Rosary College had no theatre, just a gymnasium with a small stage at one end. During the war, David B. Itken and Sidney Breese had come every summer to stage *Midsummer Night's Dream* in the college quadrangle, and because of Rosary's close connection with the Goodman School, I was almost assured the one semester position.

In a way this job became a dream-nightmare because I hadn't acted in almost six years; there were no class textbooks, so I had to gather up and review all my Goodman materials to create my own teaching manual instead. Also, the gymnasium's small stage had no proper spotlights, just a few indifferent overheads. The semester began in February and my teaching duties included acting, directing, and play production. Besides acting I taught costuming, stagecraft, theatre history, mixed media, and radio production. Sister Gregory taught public speaking, voice and diction, although later I taught those subjects too.

Of course, I was used to the caliber of acting students found at the Goodman, whereas the Rosary girls didn't catch on quite so quickly. For example, I had to explain and demonstrate what pantomime was. However, we soon had a nice rapport going and I can remember our theatre class sprawled in a circle on the gymnasium floor when Sister Gregory walked in, did a double take and said, "Keep up the good work, Mr. T.!" and breezed out again.

Our first play production was *Moor Born* about the Bronte' sisters, and I played the part of Branwell, the drunken brother. Casting was always a problem at an all girls' college, and I used to beg the students to invite their boyfriends, brothers, or anything remotely male to participate in the plays. Part of my job description was also set design, and I ended up building all the sets and scenery myself.

I was just 29 years old and fairly handsome when I began at Rosary, and once the nuns learned that I was going with Margaret Porter, who was also a violinist and music teacher, they took me aside for a serious talk. "You may not realize this, Mr. T., but there are 700 healthy young Catholic girls here who are *just dying to find a man*! Our advice to you is you better get married *as soon as possible*!!!" I had already been contemplating something of the sort, so one Saturday I took Margaret to Springfield to meet Aunt Faye, who took to her immediately. The following weekend we went by train to Creston, Iowa, to see Margaret's parents. Margaret's mother, Pauline Porter, was a staunch Methodist and in her eyes I was a little bit suspect as a suitor to her daughter. After all, I was an actor and there was something about "that evil business of the theatre" plus the fact that in her mind I was "rather worldly" having traveled halfway around the globe during the war. Even though I was now teaching at a Catholic college and also teaching Sunday school at Downers Grove Methodist Church, I was not what she had imagined for her daughter. Nevertheless, I proposed to Margaret, and she accepted me, although perhaps the thought of my daily contact with those nubile students gave added impetus for her to set the wedding date.

Margaret and I were married on June 15, 1946, in Creston, Iowa, and we spent our honeymoon at Hewes Kirkwood Lodge in the Colorado Rockies. Our grand adventure together, which has endured for almost 57 years, had now begun!

The nuns were satisfied with my teaching and asked me to return that Fall as a full time instructor. Through the Army GI bill I had the opportunity for further schooling and I needed a master's degree to teach at the college level.

When I asked Dr. Gnesin's advice on which theatre school to attend, his recommendation was either the University of Michigan or Yale so I chose the University of Michigan at Ann Arbor. I attended during the summers of 1946-49, and graduated with an MA in Theatre.

That first summer at Ann Arbor I met Thor Johnson, the founder of the Peninsula Music Festival. I had taken a course in costuming and was the assistant costumer for the Smetana opera, *The Bartered Bride*, which Thor was conducting, and when I mentioned to him that my wife, Margaret, was a fine violinist, he invited her to play in the orchestra. In 1953, the first season of the Peninsula Music Festival, he asked me to be the narrator of a Stephen Foster song cycle.

During that first summer in Michigan, Margaret and I rented rooms in a private house overlooking Whitmore Lake not far from the university, so we spent many happy hours lolling in the lake's cooling waters.

My professors during the eight-week summer session were Valentin Windt, Clarabel Baird, and Dr. William Purdue Halstedt, the author of the excellent book, *Stagecraft and the Elements of Theatre*. Professor Windt was very knowledgeable about directing, but I soon came to the strange realization that *I had more theatre experience than any one of them*! Because I already knew how to act there was no need for me to take acting classes—in any case I had already had superior training at the Goodman. However, I did study costume design, theatre history, aesthetics, philosophy, English and radio. During my four summers there I appeared in a play each year at the university's Mendelssohn Theatre: *Pigeons and People* by George M. Cohan, *On Borrowed Time*, *Candida*, and *The Late George Apley*.

In the fall of that year, 1946, I began my long association with Rosary College. It had started as a temporary stint but it lasted for the next 27 years! The campus exuded an atmosphere of serene academia with its Gothic architecture and quiet cloistered quadrangles. It was the Catholic Vassar of the Midwest, efficiently staffed by one hundred cheerful nuns and a comfortable assortment of Irish groundskeepers. My class load was 15 hours in a 4-day week. The nuns were always very kind to me, and when I'd have a late afternoon or evening play rehearsal they'd urge me to have supper there. "Come on, Mr. T., there's plenty of food…sit down and eat with us!"

When my last class was over and a hazy sun filtered through the leaded glass windows, I enjoyed taking an afternoon stroll around the neighborhood. River Forest had impressive homes and Tony "Big Tuna" Accardo lived just down the street. Occasionally I'd see a black sedan in the driveway and the driver would smile rather pleasantly at me, but you knew they had a gun handy so I kept walking. The nuns were always invited to the big Mafia funerals. I guess they lent a certain ecclesiastical tone, and the families liked to have them there to bless the body. Meanwhile, at the edge of River Forest lay the tangled wilderness of Thatcher Woods Forest Preserve, conveniently handy for any late night interments.

My sister Eleanor had married Wilmer Moyer in the summer of 1945, and they lived in Petoskey, Michigan, where he had a position as an organist and choral director. My father moved to California in 1946 to care for his brother Elwin, who was going blind, and in 1950 my father died of a sudden heart attack. Consequently, Margaret and I now had the family home in Downers Grove to ourselves. Our first son, David, was born April 20, 1947. Besides teaching at Rosary, I was also directing plays at the Downers Grove Civic Theatre, and directing the annual Lions Club minstrel shows. However, these shows, which traditionally had been done in blackface, came to an abrupt end when the local NAACP chapter sent a terse letter suggesting that these stereotypes were offensive and should be discontinued.

Margaret and I celebrated our first wedding anniversary at the elegant Empire Room of the Palmer House. Dressed to the nines, we drove first to Oak Park, and from there we took the elevated train into Chicago. My salary at Rosary was $2,500 a year and Margaret had quit her teaching job to stay home with our son, so money was tight. The celebrated flamenco dancers, "Velos and Yolanda", were performing that evening, and as we glanced around at the fashionably dressed clientele we felt a little nervous. However, our very kind waiter soon put us at ease when he expertly guided us to the more moderately priced entrees on the menu. Cocktails were expensive too, so we limited ourselves to one drink each and then proceeded to enjoy the rest of the evening with its fiery Spanish dancing and luxurious atmosphere. We had made sure to set aside 50 cents for the train ride home, but when the bill arrived we had not counted on an additional $8 cover charge for entertainment. I remember going through every pocket and Margaret routing desperately in her evening bag to come up with any spare change. The bill came to something like $30, the waiter did not get the big tip he might have hoped for, and counting our pennies we had just enough for the elevated train back home!

At Christmas time 1947, I brought Margaret and our baby to Rosary for a holiday party where David was much admired and fussed over by the nuns. However, when we left the festivities I slipped on an icy sidewalk and, in an effort to hold onto the baby, I fell awkwardly and broke my ankle. In those days Rosary offered no health insurance, but fortunately I had purchased my own policy just two weeks before. All my hospital and surgeon's fees were covered, and the insurance company couldn't claim it was a pre-existing condition!

Our next two children were Kathryn, born August 6, 1949, and Don, born November 11, 1951, and our lives became very full and busy indeed. All our children were later involved in scouting. I was a cub master and Margaret a den mother. They all were musical: David played clarinet and drums; Kay the flute; and Don the trombone, bass horn and guitar. Kay was a fine dancer and now teaches ballet in Pensacola. Margaret taught violin privately and was the concertmistress of the Western Suburban Symphony at La Grange from 1947 to 1990. Both boys were on a ski team in Northern Michigan so our weekends were busy too. Every summer during their childhood, we took a camping trip. Because my salary was minimal, tent camping was all we could afford, and during the next twenty years we camped in National Parks in every state in the U.S. and also in Nova Scotia and Vancouver. I loved planning the itinerary and organizing the supplies needed for these trips (my old boy scout training)! It was only when the children reached college age that they realized that many kids their own age had never been outside of their home state.

In 1953, Rosary College built a magnificent new auditorium, and this finally made it possible to present first-rate theatre productions. The structure had a 35- foot wide proscenium stage, which was second in size only to that of the Chicago Civic Opera House, and could seat 1,200. The theatre was part of a 99- room fine-arts complex which also included a music hall, music library, 20 studios and practice rooms, costume and fitting rooms, three radio booths, a two- story scene shop, a four-story high stage, classrooms, and faculty offices— all for a cost of $2.5 million!! To celebrate the grand opening of this splendid auditorium we mounted Victor Herbert's operetta, "Sweethearts" with a cast of singers and dancers drawn from not only Rosary, but also from Loyola, De Paul and the Goodman, and the lead tenor came from the Julliard School in New York City! Two of the boys in the chorus were teenage brothers from Downers Grove, Roe and Sherrill Milnes. Sherrill had studied violin with Margaret since he was seven. He was from a musical family: his mother, Thelma Milnes, was a choral director and piano teacher and a good friend of Margaret's. Sherrill became the famous baritone who sang with the Metropolitan Opera for thirty-four years from

1965-1997. In his recent autobiography, *American Aria: Farm Boy to Opera Star* published in 1998, he pays tribute to Margaret's early influence on his musical career, and now she wishes she had saved the dirt from his shoes when he was her student over 50 years ago!

In the spring of 1953 I received an invitation from Caroline Fisher Rathbone to return to the Peninsula Players that summer as actor/director. Her brother Richard had important commitments in Hollywood and Leo Lucker, their resident director since the beginning, was now acting on Broadway. I spent the next five summers at the Players, and all my children have delightful childhood memories of playing and swimming along the rocky shores and watching the nightly shows on the hillside behind the audience in their pajamas. But I will talk more about those wonderful summers at the Players elsewhere in this book.

With the new Rosary College auditorium, I could finally stage productions of the highest quality. We had a "state of the art" Izenour electronic switchboard that could be programmed to change the stage lights automatically. We did three plays a year, and over the next twenty years that added up to quite a lot of plays, so I'll merely list a few here:

Death Takes a Holiday	*Time Out for Ginger*
Night Must Fall	*The Late Christopher Bean*
Importance of Being Earnest	*The Late George Apley*
Trojan Women	*Mad Women of Chaillot*
Electra	*Dear Brutus*
The Crucible	*Sabrina Fair*
A Delicate Balance	*Light Up The Sky*
Diary of Anne Frank	*The Righteous Are Bold*
Song of the Scaffold	*The Lady's Not ForBurning*
Our Town	*The Chester Mystery Cycle*

Over the years I had a number of talented theatre students. Two of them, Pat Requa and Joan Pat Schowalter, I brought along with me to the Peninsula Players in 1953 as apprentices. Sonja Lanzener is now associated with the Alabama Shakespeare Festival, and Margaret and I visited with her this winter.

Megan Cavanagh's mother, Jonni Walsh, was a drama student of mine, and Megan performed both at the Peninsula Players, American Folklore Theatre, and Door County's Comedy Cabaret was founded by Amy McKenzie and Megan. She now works in Hollywood. At times I have suggested to my more talented students that if they are serious about theatre they should go to the Goodman, which would offer them more in-depth training for the theatre.

Rosary had become a second home to my family and me. My children played bit parts in plays and were included in all the Rosary Christmas programs. As my workload increased, I was fortunate to hire the very talented David Morrison as stage designer. He not only built sets but also helped me build my new kitchen cabinets in the scene shop in our spare time. David later became the scenic designer and director at Pheasant Run Playhouse in St. Charles.

Now commenced a very exciting period where I began to lead a double life, so to speak. Besides full time teaching at Rosary, I began to perform regularly in Chicago theatres like Salt Creek Theatre, Tenthouse Playhouse, Drury Lane Theatre, Melody Top, Pheasant Run, and Mill Run Playhouse. All of these summer theatres operated with a "star" system. In other words, a famous but slightly past their prime Broadway or Hollywood actor would be hired for big bucks ($5,000 to $10,000 per week) to attract a large audience, and then the rest of the cast would be local Chicago actors.

One of my first plays at Salt Creek Theatre in Hinsdale was *Bus Stop* by William Inge starring Barbara Baxley and Sidney Blackmer, which was staged in 1957. Other performances at the same theatre included *Inherit the Wind* in 1958, where I played the Reverend Jeremiah Brown, and *The Royal Family* (about the Barrymore family) starring Linda Darnell in August 1959. I played Dr. Chumley in *Harvey* starring Joe E. Brown as Elwood P. Dodd at the Tenthouse Theatre in June 1959 in Highland Park.

In 1960 I began a very satisfying relationship as resident character actor at Melody Top Theatre which presented fantastic musicals like *Brigadoon, Annie Get Your Gun, Oklahoma, Kismet, South Pacific, King and I, Carousel, Kiss Me Kate, Silk Stockings, Vagabond King,* and *Bells are Ringing* with such stars as Dennis Day, Genevieve, John Raitt, Jaye P. Morgan, Sheila and Gordon MacRae, Howard Keel, Phil Ford and Mimi Hines, Earl Wrightson and Lois Hunt, and Bob Newhart. The Melody Top itself was a huge tent, a theatre in the round that seated 1,500, with state of the art lighting and sound systems, and a live orchestra.

Weather always lent a bit of excitement to the productions. I vividly recall the opening show *Oklahoma* starring John Raitt in June 1960. During the final rehearsal the skies suddenly turned black and it looked like a tornado was coming. The cast was nervous and I remember talking to some old roustabout in charge of the tent who assured us that the mammoth structure, anchored by foot-thick steel cables, would probably be all right. The storm's fury left a terrible mess of upturned chairs and debris, but several hours later the show went on as planned. One of the financial backers was Chuck Comiskey of the Chicago White Sox family and the theatre was so successful that in 1963 they built a second Melody Top in Milwaukee. We usually did a two-week run in Chicago and then took the show to Milwaukee for the next two weeks.

I would never classify myself as a singer or dancer yet I could hoof it up with the best of them; twirling a hat or cane was no problem. To reach the Melody Top center stage, you had to run down an 80-foot aisle to the bottom of the tent. I always made sure my children had aisle seats and as I swept past them at the end of a scene, I'd give them a nod or tip of my hat. I remember a production in 1963 of *Vagabond King* with the magnificent voices of Earl Wrightson and Lois Hunt. The performance also included two ballet dancers from the American Ballet Theatre—Ruth Ann Koesun and John Kriza. Our daughter, Kay, was a young ballet student then but I don't think she realized how famous these dancers were until years later. For several seasons, Earl Wrightson was a favorite at the Melody Top and I enjoyed talking with him. Originally from Baltimore, his father was a Methodist minister and he was the youngest of eight children. Sadly, perhaps from over-expansion, the Chicago Melody Top went bankrupt in 1966 and I was present at the "wake" when all the lights, chairs and equipment were sold at auction for peanuts.

In summer 1966, I was invited to direct four productions at the Country Playhouse in South Bend, Indiana: *Sound of Music, South Pacific, Carousel,* and *Funny Thing Happened on the Way to the Forum.* I auditioned the casts, which were drawn from Chicago performers. Margaret played in the orchestra for some of the productions; and because we didn't want our 15 year-old son Don to be at loose ends and unsupervised for six weeks, we enrolled him at Culver Military Academy summer camp, which was 35 miles south of the playhouse. Within a week our daughter Kay was getting pitiful letters from Don imploring her to *"Please tell Mom and Dad to come and get me out of this hell hole!"* Poor Don thought he had been exiled to prison camp because the military influence required him to make his bed over and over again until all wrinkles or creases were gone. However, the experience wasn't all dreadful because he learned to sail that summer and he played in the Culver marching band on the State Capitol steps in Indianapolis for U.S. President Lyndon Baines Johnson.

In September 1968 I played Kathy Crosby's father in *Sabrina Fair* at the Mill Run Theatre, and received my first Jeff award as Best Supporting Actor in the part of Linus Larrabee. Kathy, wife of Bing Crosby, besides being a lovely actress, was also a registered nurse and schoolteacher, so she was completely down to earth. At the time, I drove a green Triumph Spitfire, a cozy two-seater, which I lovingly called "my little French mistress" because it was high maintenance—every month it needed a bit of expensive work at the garage. On our days off from the theatre it was a delight to drive Kathy and her eight-year-old daughter Mary Frances around Chicago, where we visited the Museum of Science and Industry and the lakefront. The Spitfire was a romantic car, built to meander along English county lanes but not to do battle with Chicago expressway traffic. One day I arranged a reception for Kathy at Rosary College where we performed a scene or two from *Sabrina Fair* and other readings, which delighted my students and the nuns. Kathy sent Christmas cards to Margaret and me for the next five years, and her daughter Mary Frances went on to star in the TV series *Dallas*. She was the woman who shot J.R. Ewing!

I had done some television and radio commercials over the years but my most lucrative spot was for Purina Dog Chow in 1965, where I played a mailman with a dog at my heels. It was aired for 2 or 3 years on the Danny Kaye, Jackie Gleason and Sid Caesar shows, and I received residuals of $5,000 to $6,000 a year, which was equal to my salary at Rosary! Another commercial was for the Sears Bank, where I was depicted as a pipe smoking John Neill, successful retiree who invested his savings at Sears Bank. A full-page ad of John Neill happily painting at an easel at the lakefront appeared regularly in the Chicago Tribune. People often recognized me on the train and asked, "Aren't you John Neill?" High visibility, but it didn't pay much.

Sister Gregory, my Rosary colleague, had many theatre contacts beyond the cloistered walls of the college. Mary

Martin was a good friend and had used Sister Greg's ecclesiastic advice to add authenticity when staging *The Sound of Music*. Her other famous friends included Oscar and Dorothy Hammerstein, Hume Cronyn and Jessica Tandy, and Florence Henderson. She had a terrific sense of humor, and one of our memorable collaborations occurred at a cast party following a theatre performance. I have a passing acquaintance with the piano, playing mostly by ear. Sister Greg and I put on a nightclub act together where she'd lean, boozily, against the piano holding a martini glass filled with water and an olive, pretending to be an inebriated chanteuse, while I tickled the ivories. The students loved it!!

When I was in a show at the Ivanhoe or Candlelight Theatres, the nuns used to come, en masse, to see me perform. I would gaze across the footlights and see a flock of penguins who took up a entire row. Wednesday was my day off at Rosary so I could perform in matinees. My theatre classes were usually in the afternoons because if I were in a Chicago play, I'd get home after midnight and sleep late. My students loved Mondays because I regaled them with stories about the stars I had performed with the previous week. The nuns paid for all my children's college tuitions, or what it would have cost, had my children attended Rosary. David graduated from Indiana University, Kay and Don graduated from Western Illinois at Macomb.

In 1970, 85% of the faculty at Rosary was nuns. It was the first year the college had gone co-ed, admitting three male students who were going to live on campus. I remember attending a faculty meeting where there was terrible consternation amongst the nuns as to how they were going to safeguard their girls whose virtue had been entrusted to them. I had been at Rosary for over twenty years by then so the nuns knew me well. At one point, the discussion became so ridiculous that I finally blurted out, "Sisters, set your mind at rest about any possible improprieties! What you need to do is segregate these three male students at the farthest end of one of the dorms and then install a chain link fence across the hallway to keep the girls out *and the boys safe*!! This got a big laugh!

In 1971 I was appearing in a rather avant garde play at the Ivanhoe Theatre called *Status Quo Vadis* by Donald Driver, which was a tremendous success and ran for over a year. I played the part of Father Mathais, a Catholic priest, and by all indications this production was headed for Broadway.

I had been at Rosary College for 27 years, and was a full professor at the very top of the pay scale—*$15,000 a year*! I was 55 years old, and one day the nuns took me aside and said, "Mr. T., you're working yourself to death here, you're doing 40 weeks of theatre plus full time teaching…maybe you should consider retirement!" And in a way they were right, because I was doing so much theatre work that I barely had time to teach! So with Margaret's help, I made the decision to retire and spend the rest of my life pursuing my acting career. All my kids were out of college and grown up, so I had no further responsibilities there. Both my parents had died at age 65, and I just assumed that I would too. I had just ten more years left, or so it seemed, and it made perfect sense for me to spend them doing what I loved. What I didn't know, of course, was that instead of ten, I would have *another thirty years in the theatre*!

So, thanks to the nuns, I made the decision to retire and to leave the safety of the beautiful Rosary College campus. "Goodbye, Mr. T…God bless you!" And at fifty-five, I was a free man again; *I was out of the nunnery*!

Chapter 9
Chicago Theatre World

The long running play, *Status Quo Vadis*, had opened at the Ivanhoe Theatre on August 27, 1971 and a year and a half later it was still going strong! The audiences loved it, and in the words of the theatre critic William Leonard, "Little wonder that this is a show Chicago has taken to its heart…it's both bright and bawdy, making some sage points about human relationships expressed in naughty words, crammed with real life characters, bubbling with mirth and simmering with seriousness!" (*Chicago Tribune*, November 21, 1971)

It was a rather unusual play with no scenery, and it was performed in the round, which provided intimacy and a powerful audience connection. Its medium was satire: a vitriolic comedy on class structure and prejudice where, to denote their status in society, all the actors wore numbers on their costumes. By the end of November, critic Leonard had written, "There are rumors that the New York producers want to buy the rights and take *Status Quo Vadis* to Broadway… Obviously, the money boys are nibbling on this tasty little morsel of bait!"

It appeared that my decision to retire from Rosary College had been the correct one because *finally*, after a thirty-year hiatus, *I was actually going to be performing in a play on Broadway*!

Prior to Broadway, *Status Quo Vadis* played for a week in Wilmington, Delaware at the Playhouse Theatre, starring Bruce Boxleitner, Gail Strickland, and newcomer Ted Danson who played the bartender (this was several years prior to the TV series *Cheers*). We had enthusiastic audiences and great reviews!

After six preview performances, we opened February 22, 1973 at the Brooks Atkinson Theatre, 47th and Broadway, and as the curtain fell after the final act, we were given a standing ovation with at least ten curtain calls! Even the stagehands were excited, and the buzz from the box office was that it would be a hit! After the show we wandered over to Sardi's Restaurant for a few celebratory drinks to await the newspaper reviews which usually came out about midnight. The first was from Clive Barnes of the *New York Times*, a rather tepid review which called the play "a moderately amusing comedy of social comment from a small theatre in Chicago;" we weren't unduly concerned, however, because our previous experience was that it took time to build audiences. To lighten our spirits, the playwright, Donald Driver, and the producer, George Keathley, both assured us that no matter what, we had enough money in the bank for at least a two-week run!

When we arrived the next day for the matinee, however, a big sign on the door said *"Theatre Closed"*! Apparently, the box office had sold only eight tickets for that day, and the decision had been made to close the show! We were all in shock and George Keathley assured us that the producers were very sorry but they really couldn't take any chances. Later Geraldine Kay, who had won a Jeff award for her role in *Status Quo Vadis* and who was also a native New Yorker, confided to me that the investors were connected with a very successful Connecticut playhouse and were probably using this play as a tax loss to offset profits from their other venture! During this same period, the mega-hits *Jesus Christ Superstar* and *Grease* were electrifying Broadway, so we had very stiff competition!

A few days later, as Margaret and I were driving back home along the Pennsylvania Turnpike, we heard someone on a New York talk show comment, "It's too bad that cute show *Status Quo Vadis* closed—it was really hilarious!" Well,

Broadway is a very fickle mistress and my reaction to the whole experience was "To hell with it!!" I could honestly say I had opened on Broadway, and nobody had to know the play lasted only one night!

The Irish dramatist Hugh Leonard had chosen the veteran actor John McGiver to star in the premiere of his brilliant play, *Da*, in 1973 at the Dublin Theatre Festival, and I was fortunate to have played with McGiver at its Chicago premiere at the Ivanhoe Theatre in January 1974. John McGiver had the type of face that everyone recognized, but no one knew his name. A former high school teacher and later drama professor at Catholic University in Washington D.C., he was a good family man with ten children. We had much in common because he, too, had supported his family by teaching. Prior to this we had worked together at the Ivanhoe in December 1970 in Dalton Trombo's macabre comedy, *The Biggest Thief in Town*, about a small town undertaker (McGiver) and the corpse of a rich old skinflint whom everyone had hated. The part of McGiver's daughter was played by a young Shelley Long.

The central characters were the town doctor, the newspaper editor (me) and the undertaker who plot to arrange a very expensive funeral for the deceased, who is now lying in the coffin, center stage. Meanwhile, the three central characters are trying to compose a favorable obituary for this nasty old man whom everyone had disliked. The corpse was played by 90 year-old actor, Jack Reidy, whose only job was to recline in the coffin and then, at the proper moment, raise his arm because, in fact, the old skinflint had not died but was merely unconscious!

Much to our chagrin, Jack had fallen asleep and no amount of talking, even when leaning over the open coffin, could rouse him! We finally had to kick the coffin to wake him and by this time the audience knew something was fishy. In the end, when his tremulous arm rose slowly from the coffin, rather than shocking the audience, it got a big laugh! However, this happened only once, because from then on Jack Reidy made sure he napped at home *before the evening performance*!

But I think the strangest production I was ever involved with was when Lee Bouvier, Jackie Kennedy's sister, starred in *The Philadelphia Story* at the Ivanhoe in July 1967. There had always been quite a bit of sibling rivalry between the two sisters, I believe. Jackie was married to the U.S. President and later, after his assassination, to the richest man in the world, whereas Lee Radziwill's husband was only a minor Polish prince. Lee spent her time with the "glitterati" but in recent years she had artistic friends like Rudolf Nureyev, Margot Fonteyn and Truman Capote, and when she compared herself to these creative people she began to wish that she, too, had some yet undiscovered inner gift. Kitty Carlisle Hart had casually mentioned to her that she might look marvelous on stage, so Lee made up her mind to become an actress. Through connections in the entertainment world it was suggested that first she must take some acting lessons, so she studied voice and diction for a year and a half with a drama coach at the London Academy of Music and Dramatic Arts. Eventually, a theatrical agent found her a starring vehicle in *The Philadelphia Story*, that charming play by Philip Barry, which in the movie version featured Katherine Hepburn, Cary Grant and James Stewart. The role of Tracy Lord, a beautiful but spoiled post-debutante from an aristocratic East coast family, seemed to be tailor-made for Miss Bouvier. She had rehearsed her lines with a London drama coach and her costumes were being designed by Ives Saint Laurent.

I was hired to play her father, Seth Lord, and C. K. Dexter Haven (the Cary Grant role) was played by John

Ericson, a handsome guy who had starred opposite both Elizabeth Taylor and Grace Kelly at MGM; therefore, Miss Bouvier's acting debut was cushioned by a cast of seasoned professional actors. The play, directed by Sidney Breese, was scheduled for a month's run in Chicago; and I remember we were all very impressed when at the first reading of the script, Miss Bouvier already knew her lines, word perfect! None of the actors had worked in the round before and after a while I suggested to Sid Breese that while he concentrated on directing the other actors, I could work with Miss Bouvier, teaching her where to move as she spoke her lines. She was grateful for my help because she had never acted on stage before, let alone in a leading role, and *she was absolutely scared to death*!

During rehearsal, I had noticed this strange pasty fellow slumped in the back of the theatre, and whenever Lee spoke her lines he made these little cooing noises, and I only gradually realized that this was her mentor, Truman Capote. After a week her husband Prince Radziwill turned up at rehearsals, and one day he took me aside and quietly asked my opinion.

"Do you think she'll make an actress?"

I answered him, "Yes, she has a theatrical presence about her, a certain aura, but she needs more training."

I jokingly suggested that besides further training, she also needed to appear in a venue where nobody knew her— like East Cupcake, Iowa—where she could gain some stage experience, anonymously!

Opening night was an absolute circus; it was the biggest event Chicago had ever experienced in terms of publicity. The street in front of the theatre was blocked off with policemen everywhere and was ablaze with klieg lights like a Hollywood premiere! Even the theatre entrance was cordoned off, and I had to show identification to prove I was a member of the cast. Every TV station and newspaper within a 100-mile radius was there, jostling for photographs and a big story!

The reviews the next day were relentless, the most memorable being Richard Christiansen of the *Tribune* who said, "Lee Laid a Golden Egg", and called her acting "wooden and stilted with awkward posture and a voice of extremely limited range." And he was correct because Miss Bouvier's delivery of her lines never varied from that very first day of rehearsal, her character development never deepened, and she never learned to interact with her fellow players. However, that mattered little to the sold-out audiences who, during the month-long run, came in droves to gawk at her costumes by Ives Saint Laurent, her bouffant hair by Kenneth, and her make-up by George Masters of Hollywood. She was a sweet girl, and I felt sorry for her, but she was no actress!

In 1975 I received my third Jefferson award for a cameo role in *Raisin in the Sun* written by Lorraine Hansberry and starring Claudia McNeil, who was reprising her role from the original 1959 Chicago and Broadway premieres starring Sidney Poitier and Ruby Dee. Miss McNeil was a powerful actress, as was the all-black cast who appeared in the June 1975 Chicago's Forum Theatre production. The play's title was taken from Langston Hughes' poem, which begins, "What happens to a dream deferred? Does it dry up like a raisin in the sun?"

I was cast as a bigoted, white real-estate agent who tells the family who are buying their first house, "You shouldn't move into this neighborhood...it would be better if you moved into this other neighborhood where you'd be happier with your own kind!" I had just this one scene and as I spoke these lines to the family, I was given such a look of pure animosity it was like being struck with a blow! I sensed they weren't acting but just reacting to words they had possibly experienced in their own lives. In fact, in rehearsals I had great difficulty learning my lines because one glimpse at those hateful stares, and my mind went completely blank. Finally I memorized my lines, but offstage I was never a member of the group...I was firmly excluded.

One night during the run, I got a note from the box-office that said, "Joyce and George Gibbs are here to see the show and would like to see you afterwards." I said to myself, "Who are Joyce and George Gibbs?"... For the life of me I couldn't think who they were! So I telephoned Margaret to ask her and she said, "That's Nat's sister and brother-in-law!" (My sister Eleanor's daughter, Jean, had married Nat Powell, an African-American. Theirs' was an enduring marriage and their daughter, Florida's top math scholar, won a four-year scholarship to Harvard!)

Well, of course, when they came backstage, I recognized them from Nat and Jean's wedding so I introduced them to the cast and with a great flourish I said, "Claudia, these are my relatives!" explaining that they were my niece's aunt and uncle. From that moment onward, I was accepted as *just another member of the cast*!

In *Born Yesterday*, Betty Grable played Billie Dawn, the dumb blonde girlfriend of Harry Brock, and I played his boozing attorney. The production at the Mill Run Playhouse in Niles in September 1968 was, of course, another "star venue" for a famous actress to draw in the crowds. Talk about catty reviews, one female critic described the 51-year old star by saying,

"Her chin sags, her neck does too and there are bags under her bright eyes. Her once celebrated baby doll complexion is masked by TV make-up, her arms are a smidgen heavy and her shocking pink dress is too long."

What a nasty thing to say about a gorgeous girl with still fabulous legs, whose pin-up photo graced our Air Force barracks throughout the war! If I had been interviewed for the article, I would have told them that, in middle age, *Betty Grable was a delicious little cupcake despite being heavily frosted*!

Mickey Rooney came to town to perform in the musical *Showboat* at the Arie Crown Theatre at McCormick Place in April 1974. The cavernous auditorium, which seated 5,000 people, had many acoustical problems, including an annoying echo, so that your voice floated back to you a second or two after you'd spoken. The stage itself was a hundred feet across, you had to really hustle to reach center stage in time for your number, and you just prayed that your microphone was still working!

Mickey Rooney was 54 or so, a great entertainer, but he always played the same character, which was himself. He was between divorces—he had been married six or seven times—and he was off the booze but had plunged into an emotional abyss which had brought him close to suicide. During this time, a friend had taken him to church and, all of a sudden, he got religion! I remember while we were doing the show that he'd gather all the actors together just before the performance and conduct a little prayer service right there onstage—he'd call upon God's help to bless our show because prayer had saved his life!

He was quite a little potentate. I knew actresses who had told me that when someone in the audience would arrive late, Rooney would stop the production, point to the offender and generally embarrass the person, and then start the show over again from the beginning. But the audiences seemed to love it! He was like a little elf, a show-off, always needing attention.

I appeared with Gordon and Sheila MacRae in the musical, "Bells are Ringing" at the Melody Top in 1961 and during the run I shared a dressing room with Gordon who was a very charming fellow, a great singer, and a minister's son. I remember he had a thick roll of bills of $1,000 or more, which he left lying on the dressing room table between us. I told him I'd be more comfortable if he left it with the stage manager for safekeeping during the show!

In the meantime, his wife Sheila would pose endlessly in the mirrors which lined the rehearsal hall. She knew all her lines, of course, having done this musical a zillion times before, so while the chorus rehearsed their number, she'd mouth the words while slowly turning her perfectly made-up face from side to side to determine which was her best profile. At the time, I was making $100 a week, and the MacRae's were being paid $10,000! Apparently they owed the Internal Revenue some back taxes, so they needed to earn some extra money.

In June 1959, I played Dr. Chumley in that beloved classic, *Harvey*, opposite Joe E. Brown, who starred as Elwood P. Dowd. Although he had played the part over 1500 times on Broadway, London and Australia, he had never performed in the round before. The director at the Chicago Tenthouse Theatre had been trying to get him to move around the stage more but Joe E. Brown wouldn't listen to him. So, finally, I confronted him.

"You know Joe, I was sitting in this section of the audience, and all I could see was your back...I didn't care for that view, and if I were a paying customer, I'd want my money back!! Joe, you have to move around, you have to play to the audience!"

"Okay, okay...I'll do it!" he muttered begrudgingly.

So, in the end he was grateful to me for that little bit of advice. We're in the run now and during a performance, he comes up to me, rather perplexed, and says, "You know, I don't know what's going on here but the scene we have together seems mighty short! What's the matter with this scene...why is it so short?"

So I went to get the script and pointed out to him, "Joe, you're cutting lines from this part to there, so you've cut about seven or eight lines!"

"Oh, I didn't realize that." So then he went back and played the scene as it was written.

In rehearsals he had the habit of going up to individual cast members to complain about how they had done their scene.

"Look, you didn't do this part right...you were supposed to do it this way, instead of that way!"

After comments like these, the cast was beginning to dislike him because the guy thought he was God's gift to the stage, he was acting so arrogantly. However, he seemed to like the way I played Dr. Chumley and one day he invited me out to lunch and told me he enjoyed working with me and asked if I'd like to go on tour with him in *Harvey*. I told him I was very flattered, thank you very much, but I was teaching at Rosary College and couldn't get away.

The great Joe E. Brown had a way of moving his elastic mouth so it appeared to be three feet wide! He began his career at age ten while balancing on a tightrope in the circus!

One of the most distinguished actresses I had ever performed with was Eileen Herlie in *Little Foxes* at the Ivanhoe Theatre in August 1969. Miss Herlie, a British actress, had been a member of the Old Vic Company and had played in Sir John Gielgud's Broadway revival of *Hamlet* with Richard Burton, and had also appeared in the film version opposite Sir Laurence Olivier. In *Little Foxes*, a play by Lillian Hellman about a nouveau-riche Southern family which is just filled with evil venomous characters, Miss Herlie starred as the wicked Regina Giddens and I played her aging sick husband, Horace. At the end of the second act there is a shocking scene during which Regina goads her husband into a heart attack: I then collapse onstage, and am carried off by my loyal black servant. Because the Ivanhoe was a theatre in the round, and he was not a big man, he stumbled on the step going up the aisle. I was unable to help him because as Horace, I was supposed to be either dead or dying. Eventually, he collapsed and I landed on a patron's lap in the front row, slightly bruising my side and my back on the armrest. Somehow, he picked me up again and we managed to stagger up the aisle and out of view. You can be sure this incident presented us with a huge psychological problem—what will happen the next time we do it?! The following day we practiced lifts until we felt confident it would not happen again! The production was brilliantly directed by George Keathley, and I received a Jefferson nomination for my role as Horace Giddens.

One of my very favorite shows was *On Golden Pond* by Earnest Thompson, a tender play whose message resonates even more strongly now that I am older. The setting was a lake cabin in Maine where the venerable New England couple, Norman and Ethel Thayer, have returned each summer for the last 48 years. Jim McKenzie, the late executive producer of the Peninsula Players, through his Broadway connections, was able to secure the production rights to the new play, which had its Midwest premiere at Fish Creek in the summer of 1980. Jean Sincere and I played the lead roles along with Dennis Kennedy, Jodean Culbert, Mark Maranto and Montgomery Davis, who also directed the play. I was 63 years old at the time, Norman Thayer was 80, and I thought to myself, "How do I play an 80 year old…what does he think, what does he feel?" Both my parents had died at age 65 so there was no path to follow there.

I read the script and could envision the human interactions the playwright wanted to convey. Norman was a crotchety old man, increasingly difficult to live with; he was impatient and angry about his growing frailty, and very frightened of death. He is alternately befuddled, irritable and caustic in his comments. On the other hand, his wife copes by being relentlessly brisk and cheerful, sustaining a constant birdlike chatter. Norman has been estranged from his 40-year old daughter, who suddenly appears with her fiancé and his 12-year-old son. A bond forms between them when Norman takes the young boy fishing and eventually he becomes the grandson he never had.

Jean Sincere was marvelous in this tender play, and most of the time I felt like *I was Norman*, I identified so completely with the role. After one of the performances, the aunt of the playwright came backstage and, with tears in her eyes told me that, "You're the one the play was written for— you embodied the part!" I felt very honored!

On Golden Pond then moved to Chicago, where it played six weeks at the Northlight Repertory Theatre in January and February 1981 with the original cast. After the run, Jean Sincere left the production and was replaced by Janet Gaynor.

The play then moved to the World Playhouse on Michigan Avenue with Janet Gaynor playing opposite me. In 1929 she had been awarded Hollywood's very first Oscar for her part in four movies. She was now 74 years old and cute as a lollipop; the dynamics of the play had changed, however. For example, Jean Sincere and I could argue and fight realistically not only because we were attuned to each other but because she had a sharpness, an edge. With Janet, that element was missing, she was more like biting into a caramel—soft and sweet. However, I don't think it made a bit of difference to the audiences who were comprised of little old ladies who had come to see Janet Gaynor, star of the Silver Screen. After the performances there would be long lines of them waiting to meet Miss Gaynor and get her autograph. *Nobody wanted my autograph*; not that I expected it when I was appearing with a Hollywood icon who was still cute as a button!

During the run she received an unusual fan letter, and I quote:

Dear Miss Gaynor,

We attended the Wednesday, April 15th matinee. We enjoyed you but we were overwhelmed with bewilderment at all the vulgarity the play had. We always thought of you as a very high-class sophisticated lady. Also, that child is much too young to be allowed to use that kind of language. He should be reported to the juvenile authorities!

We feel we wasted our $10 ($20 total). We could have enjoyed a nice meal in Water Tower instead.

Signed,

Adeline Smith
Pamela Brown
Chicago, Illinois

During the run, Mary Martin flew in to see Janet Gaynor, who was her long-time friend. Years ago when I saw her in "Peter Pan", I always thought of her as short, like a little elf. Imagine my surprise when I met her in person, and she was an elegant lady, almost six feet tall in high heels, with a powerful handshake! She was also a close friend of Sister Mary Gregory, who had kept her photo on her desk all the years that I knew her.

The Goodman Theatre presented a powerful production of Tennessee Williams' *Night of the Iguana* in April 1978, and I received a Jeff Award nomination for a best actor in a supporting role for my portrayal of Jonathan Coffin, a 97-year old poet. Set in a Mexican fishing village near Acapulco in the 1940's, it starred Ruth Roman as the blowsy proprietress of a seedy hotel; Barbara Rush as Hannah Jelkes, a chaste

Nantucket spinster who, along with her aging senile grandfather (me), was stranded at this shabby hotel, trying to eke out a living by selling her watercolor sketches. Alan Mixon played the pivotal role of Reverend Lawrence Shannon, a defrocked minister still hoping to rejoin the church after years of alcoholism, insanity and other unholy activities. He was dismissed from his church for fornication and heresy and now he is reduced to the shakes and a penchant for young girls.

The director, George Keathley, always had a special way with the haunted poetic loneliness of Tennessee Williams, having also directed the world premiere of *Sweet Bird of Youth* and a 20th anniversary Broadway production of the *Glass Menagerie* with Maureen Stapleton, Piper Laurie and George Grizzard. In 1969 Keathley won a Jefferson award for his Ivanhoe production of *The Rose Tattoo*.

Goodman's brilliant scenic designer, Joseph Nieminski, created a magnificent tropical atmosphere with an illusion of sweltering heat, a shabby wooden hotel, and most incredible of all—a torrential rainstorm complete with ominous thunder and an actual downpour onstage!

A week prior to the opening I was in my dressing room making up when I heard the most unearthly sounds coming from Alan Mixon's room next door...it was a terrible moaning. I had just put some lines on my face to play my ninety-seven-year-old character when I heard more strange cries so I hurried to his room to see if he needed help. When I entered, he was writhing on the floor, repeating over and over, "I've got to get out of here, I've got to get out of here!!" Suddenly, he jumped up and charged past me like a mad bull, ran out into the hallway, ran down the stairs into the Goodman Theatre, ran up the aisle into the lobby and out the door into the street. I tried to follow him, at the same time alerting the stage manager that he must do something because "Alan Mixon has gone berserk!" When I reached the lobby I saw he had run out of the theatre, crossed the tracks, and was headed north on Michigan Avenue. We were in technical rehearsals at the time and he disappeared for several days, and later was found drunk in some north side hotel room. He received good reviews for the rest of the run but I felt that in this instance he was taking the Stanislavsky method of acting too far!

He died twenty years later, at 64, of a heart attack. His obituary noted "He began performing in his grandfather's circus at age five, first as a barker and later as a tight rope walker, trapeze artist and trampolinist. He created the role of Chance in the world premiere of Tennessee Williams "Sweet Bird of Youth", and in 1957 appeared in the Broadway premiere of Williams' "Suddenly Last Summer". (*Chicago Tribune*, July 25, 1997)

I had met Tennessee Williams once when he came to the Goodman Theatre for a production of his play titled, "House Not Meant to Stand", although the piece was so awful that the theatre world re-christened it "The Play Not Meant to be Written"! On very short notice, I was asked to read for one of the lead roles and was given a copy of the script. I remember studying the part the night before, and on the train ride into Chicago the next day I was still trying to learn the lines. The play was terribly convoluted, its meaning absolutely obscure, and the dialogue impossible to decipher.

As I stood on stage reading the lines and at the same time, trying to make some sense out of them, the playwright was slumped in one of the front rows and years of alcohol and barbiturates had left him a sad wreck. In the midst of my reading, his arm suddenly shot up and he muttered, "That's not the way it was written!" and then began to read the dialogue himself. However, his delivery was nothing but inaudible, incoherent mumbling and when he was finally finished I said,

"Mr. Williams, if I were to speak the lines like you just demonstrated, no one in the audience would know what I was saying, let alone understand it!" and then I walked out of the audition!

Later, I found out that every actor in Chicago had turned it down and eventually they had to bring in a New York actor who was familiar with the play, having done it before.

My final brush with Broadway was in 1975 in *Angel Street*, a Victorian thriller written by Patrick Hamilton, and starring Dina Merrill and Michael Allinson. The 1944 movie version with Ingrid Bergman, Charles Boyer and Joseph Cotton was called *Gaslight*. Set in London about 1880, the suspense included a malevolent Mr. Manningham who is trying to drive his poor tormented wife, Bella, insane; and a crafty retired police inspector, Sergeant Rough, who is still on the trail of a 15 year old unsolved murder.

The play was a huge success on Broadway in 1941 starring Vincent Price, Leo G. Carroll and Judith Evelyn and it ran throughout the war. Its director, Shepard Traube, wanted to bring it back to life again, and thirty years later staged a version of *Angel Street* at the Arlington Park Theatre in Chicago starring Joseph Campanella and Margaret Phillips. The producers had wanted to bring someone in from Hollywood to play Sergeant Rough, but Shepard Traube had just seen me in *Charley's Aunt* with Louis Nye at Arlington Park, and he'd liked my work, so he called and asked me to read for the part. From the very beginning, the character of Sergeant Rough fascinated me—he is sly, inquisitive and relentless—it was just a very compelling role! When Traube hired me, he told me that eventually he'd like to take the play to Broadway for a revival.

The Arlington Park Theatre is in the round, a format with which Traube was completely unfamiliar. From the first rehearsal, it was very apparent that his concept of blocking the actors' movement was based on his earlier production thirty years ago. We got into several arguments but I finally convinced him to allow me to direct my own scenes, which entailed lengthy dialogue. I told him, "I want you to let me move the way I feel it!" and eventually he realized I knew what I was doing and liked my interpretation.

Shepard was an exceedingly demanding and self-centered individual whom you had to handle very carefully, because if you got on the wrong side of him, you'd never work for him again! Our two-week run at Arlington Park played to good reviews, and, I received a Jefferson Award nomination for best actor in a principle role for my portrayal of Sergeant Rough.

Several years later, Shepard called me and asked me to come to New York to begin rehearsing a new *Angel Street* production, this time starring Dina Merrill and Michael Allinson! A beautiful and gracious lady, Dina was born to great wealth—her mother was Marjorie Merriweather Post and her father, E.F. Hutton. However, Dina herself was quite unassuming and wanted to be known as an actress, a mother, and a wife (she was married to actor Cliff Robertson at the time.) Michael Allinson was a British actor who had replaced Rex Harrison in *My Fair Lady*. We opened on May 16, 1975, for a week's run at Playhouse on the Mall in Paramus, New Jersey, and received wonderful reviews, in which *Angel Street* was described as "alive and glowing". One in particular said "Robert Thompson steals the show as the inquisitive retired police inspector who will not rest until he gets his man—even after 15 long years of trying!" (*Daily News*, May 20, 1975)

Five months later, on November 12, 1975, *Angel Street* opened at Chicago's Studebaker Theatre for a month's run. Because we played over Thanksgiving, Margaret and I invited the entire cast for dinner at our Downers Grove home.

Besides our dining table, Margaret set up extra tables in the living and sun rooms, cooked two turkeys and, including our family, we were 26! We didn't have a dishwasher then so we have fond memories of Dina Merrill, wearing an apron, drying dishes in our kitchen!

Prior to our Broadway run, we played a week at the Peachtree Playhouse in Atlanta, Georgia in December 1975.

Angel Street finally made it to Broadway. We opened December 26, 1975, at *The Lyceum Theatre* in Times Square, just two doors west of the St. James Hotel where, exactly 35 years earlier, I had spent that miserable year as a starry-eyed young actor. I was now 59 years old, a retired college professor, and a family man with grown children. When Margaret and I arrived at The Olcott, our hotel just off Central Park West, an enormous poinsettia sent by Dina Merrill was waiting in our room. It was the Christmas season and Manhattan was a vast fairyland of glittery lights, festive Fifth Avenue window displays, and ice skaters at Rockefeller Center.

Angel Street opened the day after Christmas, and every evening I walked past an enormous photo of myself as Inspector Rough that stood outside the theatre. During the run, Dina invited us to her apartment, a duplex overlooking the East River, but what impressed me most was the six-foot scale model of her mother's 350 foot yacht, the "Sea Cloud", which at one time had hosted royalty like the Duke and Duchess of Windsor. Dina carefully pointed to a tiny porthole and said that when she was a child, this had been her bedroom.

The reviews of *Angel Street* by the New York critics were generally unenthusiastic. Sylviane Gold of the *New York Post*, December 27, 1975 titled her piece:

> *"The Thrill is Gone from* Angel Street. *If you'd like to be reminded of how far the theatre's come since the 40's, pay a visit to the Lyceum. That's where Patrick Hamilton's creaky suspense play* Angel Street *was revived last night—without apparent motive.*

True, the play was an enormous success in 1941...but 34 years later, Angel Street's simpleminded construction and absurd plot make it seem a naïve example of a hopelessly dated school of playmaking. In its day, it was called a psychological thriller, but last night it was obvious that the thrill was gone!"

Clive Barnes of the *New York Times* echoed these sentiments. Because of the critics' reactions and less than full houses, Shepard Traube decided to cut our salaries so I went from $750 a week to $600. Lincoln Center was close to our hotel so Margaret walked to concerts, we visited museums and saw the Rockettes at Radio City Music Hall.

The play closed on February 8, 1976, despite valiant efforts on Dina Merrill's part, who appeared on every possible television program, did endless interviews and continued to promote the play. One of the difficulties we found was that the snowstorms and extreme cold in January kept audiences away and, in the end, the investors lost $150,000. However, Margaret and I had a fantastic time in New York and *Angel Street* is a treasured memory.

Despite the New York critics' prophesy of an early demise, in January 1980 *Angel Street* rose to life again when it played at the Northlight Theatre in Evanston with Greg Vinkler as an excellent and menacing Mr. Manningham, Kathleen Melvin as the terrified Bella, and me playing Sergeant Rough again!

Chapter 10
Windy City Memoirs

Two very special theatres that enriched Chicago's cultural life for several decades were the Candlelight Forum and the Ivanhoe, and their success was shaped by the dynamic individuals who led them.

Bill Pullinsi and his friend Tony D'Angelo, the Candlelight founders, were just college kids in Washington D.C. when Bill created the concept of a dinner theatre, and in 1964, with financial backing from his grandparents, the Candlelight Dinner Playhouse was built in Chicago's western suburb of Summit. The theatre was enormously successful, producing not only serious plays but also musical comedies in its state of the art, 550-seat facility. It was also a boon to Chicago actors, directors, designers, choreographers and technical crews, who for almost forty years were provided with excellent creative opportunities. Part of the theatre's charm was it was a family-run operation. When I began acting there in 1974, I remember a short, stocky, balding man, one of Bill's relatives, who positioned himself in the lobby rather like the Godfather. To me, he was a slightly unnerving figure, but I suppose he merely enjoyed keeping track of the comings and goings in the theatre.

Another fixture for over a quarter of a century was the celebrated chef Mary Stimson, who, along with her staff, managed to serve over 500 diners a night from an imaginative menu which included such appetizers as saganaki, mozzarella and fresh basil, and crab cakes, followed by pastas, steak, fish and even lobsters, and concluded with luscious desserts! The whole Candlelight operation was a phenomenon, with Bill Pullinsi as director; his mother, June Pullinsi, as the assistant director; and his partner, Tony D'Angelo, as set designer, and stage manager. Tony was also in charge of technical staff, while Bill's grandparents Bill and Mabel Altier were financial backers, and his beautiful actress wife, Amy Silvestre, helped with play selection.

In 1972 they added the 425-seat Forum Theatre with its proscenium stage, and it was there that I acted with Claudia McNeil in *Raisin in the Sun*. The Candlelight Forum theatre operated year round with a resident acting company, and in its amazing thirty-eight year history produced over 300 shows and garnered 67 Jefferson awards! Because of its innovative dinner-theatre concept, it exposed a whole new audience to theatre who, traditionally, did not attend. The Candlelight's ambiance was rather special with its round center stage surrounded by dining tables; the waiters were always careful, however, to remove any vestiges of the meal before the show began.

Bill Pullinsi was in love with British comedies and was closely associated with the English playwright, Ray Cooney. Whenever Cooney wrote a new play, he'd contact Bill, who would then produce it at the Candlelight, and usually we'd do it at the Peninsula Players the following summer. *Funny Money*, *Out of Order*, *Tons of Money*, and *It Runs in the Family* were all zany and loony farces which were not only hilarious for audiences but also offered great opportunities for actors to "ham it up" onstage! Because the Candlelight was in the western suburbs, it was a very easy five or ten mile drive for me from Downers Grove without having to go into the Loop. The talented founder of Hubbard Street Dance Company, Lou Conte, choreographed several productions at the theatre in the 1970's.

My friend, Bill Munchow, had been a resident actor at the Candlelight since the 1960's, and in 1978 was cast as Horace Vandergelder in *Hello Dolly*. However, during dress rehearsal Bill somehow tripped on some steps, fell and broke his leg! The theatre called me immediately and said,

"Bob, can you come and do Vandergelder?"

It was August, and I was still up in Door County directing at the Peninsula Players but I agreed to do it in September. The show was terrific fun and was so popular; it was extended into November. I even got to sing a bit, and one reviewer commented that, "Bob has been hiding an extra talent—a fine baritone voice!"

During that next year, I was given all the roles that Bill normally would have played: in November-December 1978 I did *Mame*, and in January 1979 I did *Man From La Mancha*.

The Candlelight had innovative and high quality productions and over the next twenty years I appeared in the following shows:

1974   *The Real Inspector Hound*, by Tom Stoppard
        Black Comedy, by Peter Shaffer
        Solitaire, Double Solitaire, by Robert Anderson

1975   *The Good Doctor*, by Neil Simon
        The Three Cuckolds, by Leon Katz
        Raisin in the Sun, by Lorraine Hansberry
        The Gangs All Here, by Lawrence and Lee

1976   *God's Favorite*, by Neil Simon

1983   *Camelot*, by Rodgers & Hammerstein

1993   *It Runs in the Family*, by Ray Cooney
        Out of Order, by Ray Cooney

1994   *You Can't Take it With You*, by Kaufman and Hart

1995   *Carousel*, by Rodgers & Hammerstein
        It's a Wonderful Life, by Frank Capra

1996   *Funny Money*, by Ray Cooney
        Crazy for You, by George Gershwin

In June 1997, the Candlelight Forum Theatre suddenly closed its doors for good. A colorful brochure announcing their 1998 subscription season had already been printed and distributed, but apparently they had been having financial difficulties for at least a year. The final demise was quick and a shock to all concerned—especially their longtime actors, their production crew, and their loyal audience. But Bill Pullinsi commented sometime later that although the theatre closing was unfortunate, what was remarkable was that it had existed for almost forty years! In the end, it was competing against other forms of entertainment like riverboat casinos, and the times had changed. I am very grateful to have been a part of this vibrant theatre over a twenty-year period and especially to Bill Pullinsi and Tony D'Angelo for creating outstanding productions that were such a delight for Chicago audiences!!

When I was a teenager in the 1930's, the Catacombs at the Ivanhoe Restaurant on Wellington Street was the place you took your date after prom. It was there that I ordered my first real drink, "a Cuba libre", or simply rum and coke. In 1966 the Ivanhoe's owner, Richard Jansen, built a 600-seat theatre next door patterned after the successful Drury Lane dinner theatre complex of Tony De Santis in Evergreen Park, and one year later the media extravaganza of *The Philadelphia Story*, starring Lee Bouvier in her acting debut as Tracy Lord, took place at the Ivanhoe. Then in 1968 Jansen hired George Keathley, a dynamic and intelligent director with Broadway connections, and he hit the Chicago theatre scene like a bombshell! Keathley had a close association with the playwright Tennessee Williams, having produced a successful New York revival of his *Glass Menagerie* starring Maureen Stapleton, Piper Laurie and George Grizzard, and also the world premiere of Williams' *Sweet Bird of Youth*. He had a special feeling for Tennessee's emotionally haunted characters and his Ivanhoe production of *The Rose Tattoo* in 1968, starring Rita Moreno, was a huge box office hit and gained him his first Joseph Jefferson award for Best Director.

My British grandfather Edward Mealing Thompson holding me, California 1916.

My mother, Grace Van der Veer Thompson, 1914.

Mom and me, Garfield Park 1920.

My baby sister and me.

Norwood Farm vacation in Hartford, Michigan 1921.

My sister Eleanor and me in front of our Garfield Park apartment, 1926.

Alfred A. Thompson, my father.

My mother, Grace Van der Veer Thompson.

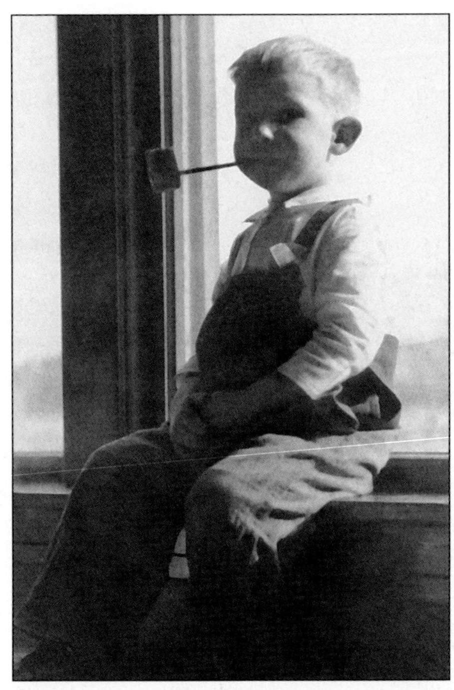

With a corncob pipe at age 3, 1 already possessed a flair for the theatrical.

Eleanor and me at the Chicago lakefront.

The beach at Michigan City, Indiana 1925.

A visit with Aunt Grace at Maywood, 1930 (Standing from left: Aunt Grace Hunt, my mother and father, Aunt Faye. Front row: myself in nautical attire and Eleanor.

My sister Eleanor in 1943.

I found "Jack" in a coalbin when he was just a pup: we were best friends for 15 years! Villa Park 1929.

About age 16.

My homemade but ill-fated kayak capsized seconds after launching!

*My flamboyant
Aunt Faye!*

*Aunt Faye at
Norwood Farm.*

Faye skiing in Colorado.

Faye loved ocean voyages and airplanes, 1947.

Aunt Faye was my inspiration for my portrayal of Lady Bracknell in The Importance of Being Earnest *by Oscar Wilde.*

At the Goodman Theatre School I played Abel Murcott in Our American Cousin, *1938.*

St. John in The Prince and the Pauper *at the Goodman's Childrens Theatre.*

Lord Windermere in Lady Windermere's Fan *by Oscar Wilde, Peninsula Players 1938.*

Various character roles with make-up inspired by Ivard Strauss

*In this foto I imagined
myself to be the next
John Barrymore!*

*"Broadway here I come!"
taken in Downers Grove
before I boarded the
Greyhound bus to conquer
New York, June 1940.*

Plymouth Playhouse in Milford, Connecticut where in 1940 I acted in summer stock.

Hilltop Theatre, Ellicott City, Maryland near Baltimore.

Home on leave, September 1943.

*Our engagement foto:
Margaret Porter and
Robert Thompson.*

Our wedding, June 15, 1946.

*Proud parents: Margaret and me
with our son, David, June 1949.*

Caroline Fisher, founder of the Peninsula Players with her parents, Lydia and C.R. Fisher.

With Maggy Magerstadt in Affairs of State, *Peninsula Players, 1953.*

As Dr. Chumley with Helen "Casey" Bragdon in Harvey, *1953.*

With June Stewart in The Lady's Not for Burning, *Peninsula Players, 1954.*

With Dr. Maurice Gnesin and Jeanne Bolan in Mr.Pim Passes By, *1955.*

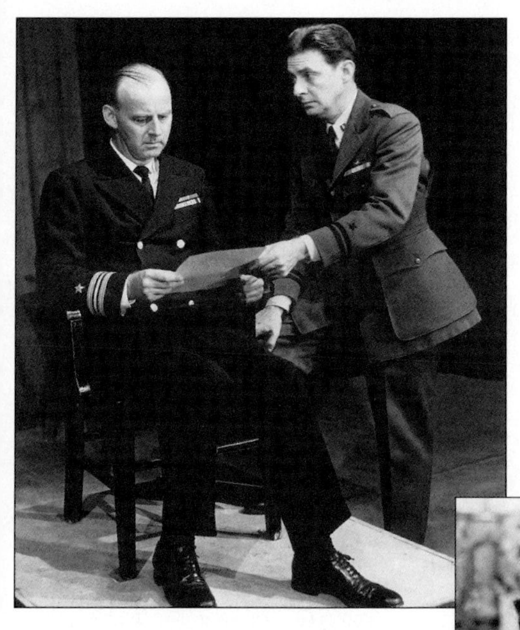

With Leo Lucker in The Caine Mutiny, *1955.*

With Linda Darnell in The Royal Family *at the Salt Creek Theatre in Hinsdale, 1959.*

From Euripides' Electra *performed at Rosary College.*

With Lee Bouvier (Radziwill) in The Philadelphia Story, *Ivanhoe Theatre, 1967.*

As Father Matthias in Status Quo Vadis, *Brooks Atkinson Theatre, New York City, 1973.*

With Kathy Crosby and her daughter, Mary Frances Crosby in Sabrina Fair, *Mill Run Theatre, 1968.*

As Sergeant Rough with Dina Merrill in Angel Street, *Lyceum Theatre, Broadway, 1975.*

With Dina Merrill in Angel Street, *on Broadway, 1975.*

My favorite role as Sergeant Rough in Angel Street.

As the mean-spirited employer "Drumm" in Da *with John McGiver, Ivanhoe Theatre, 1974.*

With Pat Fraser in Neil Simon's The Good Doctor *based on Chekhov stories, Forum Theatre, 1974-75.*

Dame Edwina Mealing makes an appearance as Lady Bracknell in Oscar Wilde's The Importance of Being Earnest, *Peninsula Players, 1985.*

Tea and Crumpets with Lady Edwina!

Amy McKenzie, Lady Edwina Mealing, and Richard O'Donnell in The Importance of Being Earnest, *1985.*

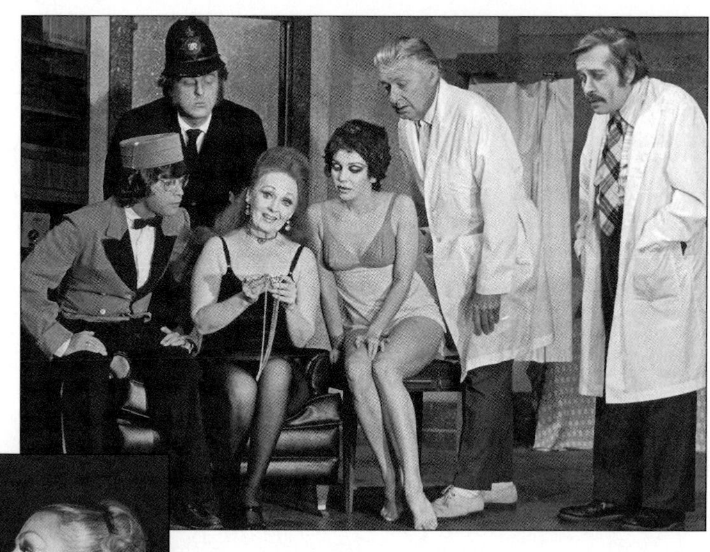

Thomas Long, ? , Mary Best, Adrian Kent, myself, Dennis Kennedy in What the Butler Saw, *Peninsula Players, 1972.*

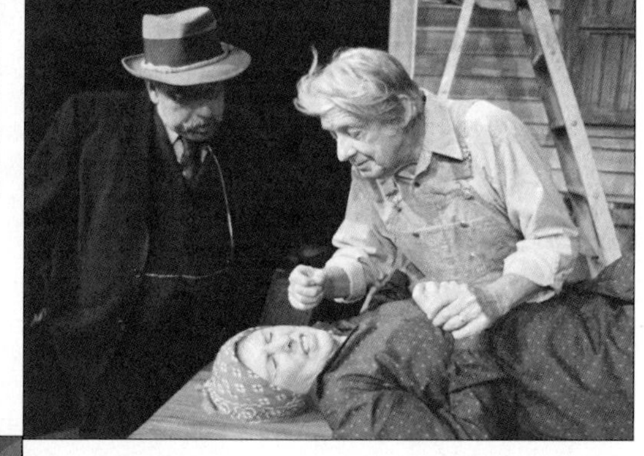

With Chris Wilson in California Suite *by Neil Simon, 1977.*

Foxfire *with Dennis Kennedy and Jean Sincere, 1983.*

Painting Churches, *1984 with Amy McKenzie, Jean Sincere and me.*

Noises Off, *1985 with Michael Tezla and Al Nuti.*

Ten Nights in a Bar Room, *1988 with Greg Vinkler.*

Lend Me a Tenor, *1991 with Amy McKenzie and Jeannette Leahy.*

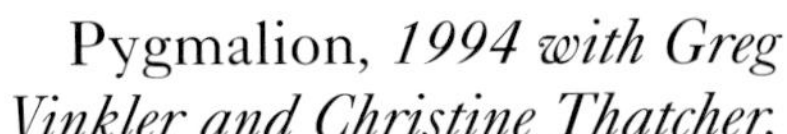

Pygmalion, *1994 with Greg Vinkler and Christine Thatcher.*

A Funny Thing Happened on the Way to the Forum, *1995 with Greg Vinkler.*

Funny Money, *1997 with Amy McKenzie and Greg Vinkler.*

Guys and Dolls, *1997 with Jacquelyn Ritz.*

Tons of Money, *1998 with Sarah Underwood, Greg Vinkler, Barbara Simpson, Karen Sheridan, and Tom Mula.*

It Runs in the Family, *1999*
with Tom Mula, Tom Kelly and
Greg Vinkler.

Over the River and
Through the Woods, *2000*
with Sharon Carlson.

A Man for all
Seasons, *2003*
*with Greg
Vinkler as Sir
Thomas More
and me playing
Cardinal Wolsey.*

Jeanne Bolan

Amy McKenzie

James McKenzie

Leo Lucker

Helen Bragdon

Dan Scott

Jean Leslie

Maggy Magerstadt

Carle Benson

Dennis Kennedy

Tom Birmingham

Jeannette Leahy

Jean Sincere

Greg Vinkler

Todd Schmidt

Tom Mula

Bill Munchow in his legendary perfor-mance as Elwood P. Dowd in Harvey, *Peninsula Players, 1950.*

Caroline and her brother Richard Fisher as a ballroom dancing duo, 1935.

Hollywood Glamour—The Fisher siblings: Richard and Margo with the newlyweds, Caroline and Rodion Rathbone, 1938.

Basil Rathbone and his wife, Ouida, with Caroline and Rodion Rathbone, Hollywood 1938.

Basil Rathbone with his son Rodion in the movie "Dawn Patrol" in 1938.

Heloise, Rodion, Rodion Jr., Caroline and Dounia in Fish Creek, 1956.

The great Shakespearean actress, Marion Foreman Rathbone.

Caroline Fisher Rathbone: dreamer, visionary, impresario, and founder of the Peninsula Players.

Bob Thompson.

At the Joseph Jefferson Awards.

Reminiscing with Bob Newhart after his appearance at the Door Community Auditorium: We had played together at the Melody Top Theatre in 1963.

Margaret and me, Downers Grove-2001.

Our children gathered one last time together at our Downers Grove home before we moved to Door County. (David, Kay, and Don)

My sister Eleanor Moyer and me, 2001.

Spouting Shakespeare in China in 1992 to a puzzled audience. Margaret told me to be quiet or I might be locked up somewhere!

Keathley was a highly imaginative and enthusiastic director. During his Ivanhoe tenure he did new plays and experimental stuff alongside the solid classics, and his productions were always of the highest caliber. Over the next few years I performed in the following plays at that theatre: *Harvey* with Tom Ewell in 1968; *Little Foxes* in 1969, (I received a Jeff nomination for my role as Horace Giddens); *Bus Stop* with Sandy Dennis, (I received another Jeff nomination for best actor in a supporting role in 1970); *Biggest Thief in Town* with John McGiver; *Another Part of the Forest* by Lillian Hellman in 1971; *Status Quo Vadis*, 1972; and *Da* with John McGiver—and for my portrayal of Drumm, I received a Jeff award for best actor in a supporting role!

Status Quo Vadis was a huge money-maker, continuing for a record-breaking 58 weeks at the Ivanhoe, but the long run seriously disrupted its subscription series and ultimately contributed to the Ivanhoe's demise. Its revenues were temporarily boosted in 1973 with another Tennessee Williams classic, *Streetcar Named Desire* starring Sandy Dennis, but the theatre closed in 1975, and Keathley moved on to become the artistic director of the Drury Lane Theatre at Water Tower Place. In the Ivanhoe's golden period, Keathley was presenting such innovative, excellent work that many of us felt he should have been the heir apparent to William Woodman, the Goodman's artistic director. However, that appointment had already been given to the very young, "fair-haired wonder," Gregory Mosher.

In November 1977, I appeared in the Goodman production of Chekhov's *The Seagull* starring Ruth Ford. It was to be the directorial debut of Mosher, whose previous credentials included a close collaboration in creating experimental theatre in north side storefronts with the budding playwright David Mamet, author of *American Buffalo*. At the Goodman, directors always have the luxury of several weeks rehearsal time, so that first week was spent reading the script. However, by the second week we were to start moving the play, getting it up on its feet. All of us were older, experienced actors, and when Mosher said, "I don't know anything about blocking a play...why don't you just move the way you feel it!" all we could do was just look at each other in disbelief!

Theatre critic Glenna Syse of the *Chicago Sun-Times* commented in her November 18, 1977 review:

"The *Seagull* wanders off course: the trouble seems to be the production does not have a definitive point of view and thus the viewer observes somewhat from afar, as if through gauze.

The company does not seem to be of one mind about mood, and a sense of ensemble is missing."

Greg Mosher spent several years as the Goodman's artistic director but then moved on to direct at Lincoln Center in New York.

In 1978, George Keathley directed another Tennessee Williams play, *Night of the Iguana*, at the Goodman Theatre. It starred Ruth Roman, Barbara Rush, and Alan Mixon, and I received a Jeff nomination for best actor in a supporting role for my portrayal of the 97-year-old grandfather.

Eventually George Keathley moved to Kansas City where he accepted a position as artistic director of the esteemed Missouri Repertory Theatre, and his long tenure there has been a happy one. In retrospect, I was very fortunate to have been a part of the superb productions when, under Keathley's inspired direction, the Ivanhoe was at the forefront of Chicago's theatre scene.

When I appeared in *The Seagull* it was actually my acting debut at the Goodman, although I would term it more of a homecoming. At age 62, I once again trod the boards of that hallowed stage where I had spent my student days. I had come full circle from Dr. Maurice Gnesin's humiliating comment, "Mr. Thompson, the object of acting is to make the audience cry, not yourself!"

And then later, in 1978, I appeared in Shakespeare's *Much Ado About Nothing* as Antonio who, garbed in doublet and breeches, cut a lively figure in scenes of swashbuckling swordplay and courtly dancing.

A final joy was participating in the Goodman's heart-warming production of *A Christmas Carol* for five seasons from 1979 to 1984, in the role of Charles Dickens, the narrator, with William Norris as Scrooge. This was truly a magnificent celebration of the Christmas spirit, and an experience I will always remember with great fondness!

Chapter 11
Peninsula Players 1953-57

Few places are as enchanting as the theatre of the Peninsula Players when capricious moonlight trans forms the woods into a scene from *Midsummer Night's Dream*. The lake is alive with moonbeams, and nymphs and satyrs might well be cavorting in the forest nearby. It's utterly romantic, yet at the same time, it can be a little sad, because the evening's performance is over, the applause is finished, and the audience has departed.

Many an evening I have lingered by that rocky shore, looking up at the stars and contemplating the vast heavens. For the past sixty-five summers, I have always returned to the Players like some homing pigeon to its roost. The Players has been one of the greatest joys of my life!

As I have described earlier, my first years at the Players were in the summers of 1938 and 1939, when I was still a student at the Goodman Theatre School. However, in the spring of 1953, while I was still teaching full-time at Rosary College and raising three young children along with my wife Margaret, I received a call from Caroline Fisher Rathbone asking me to come to Fish Creek that summer as resident actor-director. I hadn't heard from Caroline in almost fifteen years, and in the ensuing time I had tried my luck on Broadway, served in the Air Force during World War II, and had become a college professor. Caroline's brother, Richard Fisher, was working in Hollywood with CBS Television as a writer and assistant producer of the Burns and Allen Show and the Jack Benny Show, so he was no longer at the Players full-time; their founding director, Leo Lucker, was now appearing on Broadway; therefore, Caroline had need of a resident director that season. It's likely that she had also read the *Chicago Tribune* article about Rosary College's new two-million-dollar Fine Arts Building with its "state of the art" theatre, and this had given me further credibility and status.

In the 1950's the Players had a ten-week season, from late June to Labor Day, during which time ten plays were presented. It was a grueling schedule—an absolute killer because we'd be rehearsing next week's play at the same time we were performing the current play. However, there was a nucleus of very talented actors who were accustomed to working together: Helen Bragdon, Judith Haviland, Jean Leslie, Leo Lucker, Maggy Magerstadt, Bill Munchow, Maurice Ottinger, and Dan Scott. The plays were a well chosen mix of frothy comedies, suspenseful mysteries to delight the audiences, and serious dramas. We had to learn our lines quickly; I discovered one of the best methods was to study them just before bedtime. Somehow the repetition of those sentences would percolate through my unconscious all night, with the result that by morning I had substantial parts of the script memorized. It was the equivalent of sleeping with the manuscript under my pillow, and by some miracle, having the text seep through the eiderdown into my brain by osmosis!

In those days Caroline was a one-woman public relations machine. The ticket prices were quite low: the top price was $3.60 for seats near the stage and then $2.40, $1.80 and $1.20 for seats further back. There were no *Resorter-Reporter* weekly newspapers in those days so most advertising was done by laboriously placing flyers under car windshields in Fish Creek and nearby towns every week. This job usually fell to the apprentices but Caroline's three children, Héloise, Dounia, and Rodion Jr., remember this chore. Caroline herself frequently could be found standing in front of Schreiber's Store in Fish Creek, often dressed rather raffishly, and hawking tickets for the evening performance, or even giving away tickets. Despite the theatre's genteel aura and its sophisticated audiences, the Players always struggled financially. Caroline, I believe, was in the process of purchasing the theatre and property from her parents, C. R. and Lydia Fisher, who were now retiring and had moved to Hollywood, where their son Richard and daughter Margo were living. Since 1949 the devoted and sternly efficient Edith Dunn had been box office manager and was also responsible for the care of the magnificent theatre gardens.

Caroline radiated an immense personal charm; she often escorted front row patrons to their seats, treating them like honored friends (which they often were). Constantly struggling to find innovative approaches to increasing the theatre audiences, she inaugurated the idea of a showboat dinner-theatre cruise from Escanaba to Fish Creek every Saturday night aboard the cruiser "Lucky Strike" owned by Roy and Judy Jensen. I'm not sure how successful this venture was, but presumably the passengers left Escanaba sometime Saturday afternoon for a 15-mile trip across Green Bay waters, dined at the C and C Club in Fish Creek, and then were driven to the theatre in time for the opening curtain. The tricky part, presumably, was returning to Escanaba on the high seas in the dark. Normally, the wind dies down after sunset but it seems like this adventure would only be for the nautically intrepid. A few rough crossings probably put the kibosh on the venture.

When Caroline and her husband, Rodion, lived in Connecticut in 1952, she organized a show train on the New Haven Railroad that brought theatre lovers from New Haven to enjoy several Broadway plays with hotel accommodations included. In March 1956 she offered a similar show train which transported theatre goers from Escanaba to Chicago to take in three shows: *Inherit the Wind* with Melvyn Douglas, Fran Warren in *The Pajama Game*, and Burgess Meredith in *Teahouse of the August Moon*. Obviously, Caroline was committed to introducing audiences to the theatre, and a risk-taker to boot.

During the 1953 and 1955 seasons Caroline invited Dr. Maurice Gnesin, head of the Goodman Theatre, to Fish Creek to direct several plays. Age had mellowed him considerably and he was no longer the stern, demanding authority figure of my student days, but had become almost grandfatherly to my young children. Once he even called me out of rehearsal—he was quite frantic at the time and said, "You've got to come quickly, little Kay has pinched her finger!!" He was like a fluttering mother hen!

It was obvious Dr. Gnesin had never directed summer stock before, with its hectic pace and brief week of rehearsal time—at the Goodman he could luxuriate in a solid month of rehearsals. In August 1953, he was directing Casey Bragdon, Bill Munchow, Maggy Magerstadt and me in *The Late Christopher Bean* by Sidney Howard. All of us were gathered in a circle and spent the first day reading the script. The second day, Dr. Gnesin said, "All right, let's start analyzing the play a la Stanislavsky!" Meanwhile, we were getting a little nervous, inwardly saying to ourselves, "Come on, let's go, let's move it!" We kept glancing at our watches but, of course, we couldn't contradict the eminent Dr. Gnesin, head of the Goodman for the past twenty-three years! By the third day we were still on Act One; we hadn't even touched Act Three, which contained the crucial scene and pivotal point of the drama! So on opening night we were so far off and lost that we were ad-libbing all over the place, and then one of the actors completely missed his cue—it was a complete hash! However, by the following night we were much better; and on the final evening, we were perfect! A young Goodman student, Jim Maronek, who was only twenty at the time, created a marvelous stage setting that was roundly praised by the critics.

That summer I directed a whimsical AA Milne play, *Dover Road,* about an exceedingly rich man named Latimer who amuses himself by preventing unhappy marriages, and Dr. Gnesin played that role with elfin charm.

In 1955, Dr. Gnesin returned again in another AA Milne play, *Mr. Pim Passes By* and played the part of an absent-minded British eccentric. However, the reviews were mixed and one critic retitled it, "Mr. Pam Pisses By"! Sydney Harris, drama critic for the *Chicago Daily News*, July 21, 1955, who also had a summer home in Fish Creek's Cottage Row called it:

"A flimsy comedy which convulsed London audiences more than a generation ago. Somewhat less than convulsing today, "Mr. Pim" still has its mildly amusing moments, in a quaint and faded fashion.

As the wife, Jeanne Bolan proves herself of finished professional caliber...serene and spirited, she moves with a graceful economy, and manages to inject a full-blooded quality into Milne's pallid little sketch.

She is handsomely matched with Robert Thompson as the squire who embodies those traits of stupidity and benevolence, narrowness and probity, that symbolize the landed gentry everywhere—and nowhere more so than in England!

Miss Bolan and Mr. Thompson are very much the people to watch at the Peninsula Players; *and it would be a crashing injustice if they are not soon able to find their proper niches somewhere in the Broadway Theatre!*"

So in a way, I had come full circle in my relationship with Dr. Gnesin who was now in his declining years. It was he who had offered me the full scholarship to the Goodman which had provided such an excellent foundation for my theatrical career. Although he had been relentlessly critical of my student work, age had made him vulnerable and he was no longer the god-like figure I had imagined him to be, but merely human with the attendant frailties. All the years I had known him, he had smoked like a chimney, and in 1957 he died of lung cancer. Just the week before his death, I visited him in the hospital. He was no longer in control of his life, and I pitied him.

Bill Munchow was a dear friend of mine, a talented actor and a subtle comedian. He came to the Players in 1949, a graduate of Lawrence College in Appleton, Wisconsin. His legendary portrayal of Elwood P. Dowd, the tippler who is haunted by a six-foot white rabbit named *Harvey* was unforgettable, and he reprised this role in 1984 for the Players 50th Anniversary season. I played the psychiatrist, Dr. William Chumley, and Maggy Magerstadt was delightful as the snobbish society matron, Mrs. Ethel Chauvenet. Over the years Bill and I appeared together both at the Players and in Chicago theatres, notably the Candlelight Forum Theatre. Some of the memorable plays we did together in the 1950's, in addition to *Harvey*, were *On Borrowed Time*, *The Caine Mutiny*, *Mr. Roberts* and *Inherit the Wind*.

The play, *On Borrowed Time*, by Paul Osborn held special meaning for me: the story concerns a little boy, Pud (played by Eric Beckstrom) who is being raised by his grandfather (me) after the death of his parents. Pud's aunt (Maggy Magerstadt) thinks the grandfather is a bad influence on the boy, and attempts to get him away from the grandfather, thereby also gaining control of a small inheritance left to the boy by his parents. Leo Lucker played Mr. Brink (the character of Death) who has already claimed both the boy's parents and his grandmother, and is now intent on taking the grandfather's life. However, the wily old grandfather has outwitted Death so far and has tricked him into climbing an old apple tree where he is powerless. In the dramatic ending, Death lures young Pud into the tree with the promise of an apple. The child falls from a branch and lies fatally injured beneath the tree with a broken back. In this scene the heartbroken grandfather, with tears streaming down his face, attempts to bargain with Death, beseeching him to "Please take me instead, don't kill my little Pud...take me instead!!" And fifty years later, I still weep when I remember this tragic scene. I identified with it so strongly because my own little children were only 3, 5 and 7 years old at the time and I could imagine how terrible I'd feel if any of them were badly injured. Eric Beckstrom was only a young lad of 9 or 10 then, and he was splendid in the part; and Leo Lucker, as the figure of Death, was especially effective.

Inherit the Wind, performed at the Players in August 1957, was based on the infamous Scopes monkey trial with its powerful debate on evolution between attorneys William Jennings Bryan (Bill Munchow) and Clarence Darrow (me). It was directed by Leo Lucker, who had just appeared on Broadway with Paul Muni in the same play. The Scopes Trial was held in Dayton, Tennessee in 1925 where J.T. Scopes, a public school teacher, was tried and convicted for teaching Darwin's theory of evolution in violation of a state statute forbidding such instruction. To add authenticity to the play, Caroline had managed to "borrow" a rhesus monkey from the University of Wisconsin-Madison primate lab. (Caroline could get blood out of a turnip!) The monkey was kept in a cage but, being very intelligent, it managed to unfasten the cage door and escape to freedom in the surrounding woods. It was delighted with its new environment and no amount of coaxing from the cast could induce it to leave its leafy bower. Consternation reigned; what was Caroline going to do if this valuable monkey were lost! However, after a day or so without food, it voluntarily returned to its cage where a meal of its favorite fruits awaited him.

The play received triumphant reviews. Leo Lucker played the role of the bigoted preacher Reverend Jeremiah Brown, and the newspaper correspondent Henry L. Mencken was played by Harvey Korman. (We always maintained the Players had trained him for the Carol Burnett Show!)

Besides the rhesus monkey, animals have always made dramatic appearances at the Peninsula Players, wild or otherwise. I remember once being on stage when I noticed a commotion occurring in the second row. Like a choreographed Busby Berkeley number, wave after wave of patrons suddenly stood up, some even climbing onto their chairs, with a look of silent horror on their faces. I wondered what could possibly be going on, and it was only later I learned that a curious skunk had ambled along the row near the people's feet, until it finally meandered up the side aisle and disappeared into the woods.

Another strange manifestation occurred while I was rehearsing some actors in the lodge. I was facing the lake when I noticed a young woman who slowly walked across the rocky beach to the water, calmly took off all her clothes, and waded into the water naked. I didn't want to disrupt the rehearsal; and, at this point, I was the only one who could see her. On the other hand, she was no one I recognized, no errant Lady Godiva from the theatre colony. Just then one of the administrative staff came into the lodge, so I took him aside and quietly asked him to find out what was going on. I learned she was a Menominee Indian who had come to pay homage to a sacred site that was revered by her people, but when I glanced out the window again, she had vanished. And later that night, after the evening's performance, I was still haunted by this illusive vision and came to the realization that she might be just one of the enchanted woodland creatures whose spirits have helped us create the illusion of theatre.

During the Players' 20th anniversary season in 1955, Leo Lucker returned as director after touring all season in *I Know My Love* with Alfred Lunt and Lynn Fontanne. Leo was a brilliant actor and I was fortunate to have had the opportunity to work with him in 1938-39 when I was still a Goodman student. His subtle portrayal of the seemingly innocent Welsh murderer in *Night Must Fall* by Emlyn Williams, and his role as Count Dracula in the play of the same name are forever etched in my memory. Acting is a skill passed down from experienced professional to student apprentice, and I learned a great deal from watching Leo. By the late 1950's he was directing rehearsals with a thermos filled with martinis instead of coffee, and he'd become pleasantly tipsy as the afternoon progressed. However, it never seemed to affect his acting or directing ability. He retired at age 65 and lived in Manhattan, where he indulged his love of opera and theatre. It was said that when he went to collect his unemployment check, he was dressed elegantly in top hat, tails and a cane. He had been the Players' original director in 1935 and had appeared every season for almost thirty years. He died in New York City in 1977.

Sometime in the late 1940's when I was teaching at Rosary College, I attended a program given by Charles Laughton as part of North Downers Grove High School Forum Series. Perched on a stool with only a stack of books beside him, he proceeded to charm the audience for an hour and a half with his magnificent readings. As an actor, he was absolutely out of this world!

A few months later, as part of the same series, Basil Rathbone presented some sketches from Sherlock Holmes and other dramatic readings. There had always been discussions at the Players about the possibility of inviting him to appear in a play in Door County, thereby lending an air of distinction to the theatre. With Basil Rathbone making an appearance, how much better could it get? So after his program, I waited in line to meet him. When my turn came, I shook his hand and told him how much I admired his work and how wonderful he was—all the things you say on these occasions. He was very cordial but I was conscious that I shouldn't prolong the conversation because there were at least ten people waiting in line behind me. So I quickly added, "Before I go, I want you to know that I'm very well acquainted with your son, Rodion, at the Peninsula Players in Wisconsin. My wife and I are very familiar with the theatre and we love it!" The minute I referred to his son, a lightning change seemed to come over his face. It was as if a chilly veil came over his eyes, and he abruptly dismissed me with a curt, "All right, thank you and goodbye!!" and then he turned away and started talking to the next person.

I was absolutely stunned and I thought to myself, "What kind of father would not be interested in talking about his only son?"

Rodion's mother, Marion Foreman Rathbone, was Basil Rathbone's first wife and a Shakespearean actress of great distinction. A former member of the Sir Frank Benson Shakespeare Company, she was an electrifying interpreter of the great bard. In 1926, she was divorced from Basil Rathbone who had left her years before when Rodion was only four. Basil made a successful theatrical career in America, and Marion essentially raised her son by herself with the help of her family and sisters in Wales.

After World War II in 1947, she came to the Players where she gave a memorable performance as Lady Bracknell in *The Importance of Being Earnest.* I met her at the Players in 1956 or 1957. At this point her career in England was more or less over, she was close to seventy years old, and apparently Caroline and Rodion thought she might do some tutoring with the younger actors, give diction lessons, that sort of thing. Because housing was rather primitive at the Players——really just some old cabins left over from the Wildwood Camp days——a special cottage was prepared for Marion that was immediately dubbed "The Southern Mansion". It was nothing more than a former garage that had been moved down from the Buchbinder property with two Corinthian columns added to the front facade and painted white. The bathing arrangements also presented difficulties because, in the 1950's, there was just one communal bathroom shared by thirty members of the theatre colony. Consequently, half an hour in the morning and evening were set aside as "Marion's time", and this was strictly enforced.

Maggy Magerstadt Rosner has vivid memories of Marion's visit that summer:

"Marion had been a brilliant Shakespearean actress and was still capable of giving a spellbinding interpretation of her favorite roles. However, she was highly egocentric with a very needy ego; and I think when she was not the center of attention, it unhinged her. Hazel Buchbinder, who was herself an eccentric and demanding woman, perhaps the same age as Marion, was giving a small party after one of the evening performances. We were all young at the time and accustomed to walking up the hill to the Buchbinders in the dark. Marion was invited too but somehow in the confusion, no one had waited for her with the car. All the cast was already at the party and suddenly Marion burst into the room breathless from walking in the woods and her hair in wild disarray. 'My torch (flashlight) has gone out, it just failed me…and I took a little tumble but I don't think I've broken my ankle…I knew you'd all be worried about where I was. It was so late and here I was stumbling around in the brambles in the dark… Yes, at a moment like this, a whiskey would help…Just a tot, mind you, after all my travails!" (It was a wonderful dramatic entrance and a way of being sure that everyone noticed her!)

Marion was very much at loose ends that summer. Caroline and Rodion had set her up in the Wharf Gift Shop (the former boathouse from Wildwood Camp) where she sold exotic jewelry, trinkets, fabrics and art objects which Rodion, as a TWA pilot, had brought back from his trips to Saudi Arabia and Egypt. For several summers my brother-in-law, Wil Moyer a music teacher from Petoskey, Michigan, would spend a few weeks at the Players; and he became a great favorite of Edith Dunn, the bookkeeper and box office manager—a rather cranky and difficult woman who didn't get along with most people. However, Wil liked to work with numbers and figures and he helped her with the gardens, and occasionally would appear on stage in minor roles.

One afternoon while strolling through the woods Wil and I came upon a distraught Marion Rathbone slumped over on the path. She was in a terrible state, emotionally overwrought, an absolutely broken woman! Over the winter she had been living in Chicago with Rodion and Caroline somewhere in Old Town near Rush Street where she had a little gift shop. Thieves had recently broken in and robbed her of everything. She was really at the end of her tether, she felt very unconnected at Fish Creek, where her identity had suffered, and she seemed to have lost her inner compass.

Wil and I comforted her as best we could and then helped her back to her cottage. That Fall I arranged for her to give a series of readings for my theatre students at Rosary College where she was cordially received and gave a triumphant performance. And in October, my sister Eleanor and her husband, Wil Moyer, invited her to visit them for a week in Petoskey, Michigan where she was the toast of the town! I had thought that the local newspaper might interview her. Imagine the headlines: "Famous Shakespearean actress and former wife of Basil Rathbone in Petoskey!" Eleanor hoped she might give some dramatic readings at the high school, however Marion demurred. All she desired was a change of scene and a quiet rest while she enjoyed the view from their home, which sits high on a bluff overlooking Lake Michigan. She did, however, bring along some rather elegant clothing for church, and the visit seemed to give both Marion and my sister much pleasure.

In the early 1950's, my three children were quite small: two, four and six, so it was often easier and more convenient for Margaret to either stay at home in Downers Grove, or drive to Michigan to stay with my sister Eleanor, who also had young children. The cabins at the Players were quite primitive with spiders and no private bathrooms. One summer, Caroline telephoned Margaret and, unbeknownst to me, told Margaret that she had the feeling that "Bob was terribly lonely for his family and was at loose ends, emotionally. She urged Margaret to drop everything and hurry to Door County"! Well, Margaret being the good wife that she is, packed up the car with all the children's necessities and rushed to Fish Creek the following day. Of course, when they arrived I was in the midst of rehearsal and my first reaction was a rather unwelcoming "What are you doing here??" Caroline loved to play Cupid, but she also liked to exert control over people.

Margaret has commented that Caroline thrived on a crisis a day. She was always rushing off on some critical errand and once when Margaret was driving north on Highway 42 towards Fish Creek, Caroline passed her on the right hand side at considerable speed, leaving a spray of dust and gravel in her wake.

By the mid 1950's Caroline faced a major crossroad in that the cumbersome canvas tarpaulin over the audience needed major repairs or needed to be replaced with a more permanent roof. In 1956 she commissioned Neenah architect Frank C. Shattuck to design the new pavilion which exists today. Besides being water- and windproof, it would improve the theatre's acoustics. The only problem was money: there was none! The box office was always in debt and the theatre never generated the kind of income necessary to make major capital improvements. I believe the new pavilion was going to cost approximately $60,000.

I told Caroline, "You can't undertake this project because you don't have the finances to pay for this! If you do, you'll go broke, you will lose the theatre, and you won't be able to leave it to your children!"

She was absolutely furious with me and the end result was a dramatic confrontation where eventually the Board of Directors quit en masse and Caroline threw all the financial records into the bay! The theatre went bankrupt in 1960, and was purchased by New York City tax attorney Kenneth Carroad. Caroline asked James McKenzie to run the theatre, *and she never spoke to me again for the next twenty years!*

Chapter 12

Dreams, Triumphs, Disappointments

The Story of the Fisher-Rathbone Family
As told by Héloise Rathbone

My mother, Caroline Fisher Rathbone, had often described to me how she first began the theatre. When she was just nineteen, she saw a production of *Romeo and Juliet* at Northwestern University and it so moved her that she decided then and there that she wanted to create theatre. Her younger brother Richie, 17 at the time, Leo Lucker, and Stacy Keach had performed in the play. For my mother, it was one of the seminal moments of her life; she believed that the experience of theatre was terribly important because it had the power to transport the audience out of their everyday lives into the realm of imagination, ideas and emotions.

So in the summer of 1935, in the midst of the Depression, my mother and her younger siblings, Richie and Margie, drove to Fish Creek with $40 and a borrowed car. That first season the theatre was outdoors in a natural dell behind Bonnie Brook Cottage where they survived on eating applesauce made from the trees nearby. Their resources were meager but their visions were ambitious. The first plays were *Hay Fever* by Noel Coward and *Hedda Gabler* by Ibsen, and with that the Peninsula Players was born!

Mama and Papa Fisher supported their children's dream because there were not many jobs available for teenagers and what else were they going to do. A year later my mother, who was such a stunning beauty with a charismatic, appealing personality, was in the lobby of The Drake Hotel in Chicago talking to a gentleman about her vision of a theatre. By this time she had already begun her modeling career, and she and Richie performed together in night-clubs as a ballroom dancing duo. I can just imagine this vibrant and beautiful young woman describing her idea of a theatre when, inexplicably, the gentleman said,

"I'll give you $25,000!"

That's the story she told me in her later years, and I believe he gave her the check right on the spot! She used this money to purchase Wildwood Camp, the present site of the Peninsula Players. She never told me who it was but said he very much wished to remain anonymous. I can imagine that giving $25,000 to such a beautiful young woman might have seriously imperiled his marriage. As far as I know, there was no affair. Over the years he kept in touch with the theatre's activities but she had always promised never to reveal his name. Because she was under age at the time, Mama and Papa Fisher used the money to purchase Wildwood Camp.

Mama and Papa Fisher were actively involved in the theatre into the 1950's until they reached retirement age and moved to Hollywood. At this point, my mother had to figure out how to raise money to buy the theatre from her parents. When I was ten in 1952, we lived on the theatre property for 18 months and I attended grade school in Ephraim and then Fish Creek. We had a furnace but we cooked on a wood-stove. My mother had set up a corporation. I'm guessing that in those days non-profit organizations weren't as common; otherwise, someone would have told her about them. So she set up an ordinary corporation where she held the common stock, and she sold the preferred stock to people in the com-munity. She did this as a vehicle to enable her to raise money to purchase the theatre from her parents. A prospec-tus was printed and I can remember us children collating it and stapling it together. The stock was $100 a share and my mother was very involved in marketing the stock throughout the community. Ordinary people just plunked their money down. I don't know how much she had to pay her parents for the land; I was too young to know those details. However, she did eventually buy the theatre from them and the land then belonged to the corporation. To this day there are still people in the community who, when their parents have died, find a Peninsula Players stock certificate which they bring to the theatre to ask if it's worth anything.

So my mother now owned the theatre; however, the canvas tarpaulin which protected the audience from rain had begun to disintegrate. In a storm it would flap and begin to tear. I remember when I was in my teens that if you heard heavy rain during the night, it could be 2 a.m., you jumped up and ran to the theatre where there would already be twenty people pushing water out of the canvas; otherwise it would rip and break. It was imperative that the canvas be replaced and my mother envisioned a more permanent structure, the present pavilion. I think it was going to cost $40,000; and considering that the theatre would earn $500 one year and lose $500 the next, this was a risky decision. The Players was never a money-making operation so the prospect of such a major capital expenditure alarmed a lot of people. It certainly alarmed Bob Thompson. My mother believed the money could be raised by selling more stock and by obtaining a twenty-year mortgage. Somehow she'd pay it off even if it meant getting a part-time job herself.

What actually happened was something entirely different. In fact, every time I tell the story, it makes me cry. You have to understand that this was 1956 and no bank was going to consider lending money to a woman whose theatre made no appreciable profit and who was viewed as a wild and wacky artiste, besides. The theatre's board of directors was composed of men who had the right connections in the community. The beautiful new pavilion was built in 1957 with a construction loan so when the addition was completed, my mother needed to obtain a long-term mortgage. The men on the board said,

"Oh Caroline, you know the bank won't deal with you...Why don't you let one of us be board president while you become the artistic director? We'll negotiate with the bank and we won't interfere with your artistic judgment as far as running the theatre."

She agreed to do this. However, what they obtained, instead, was a three year mortgage for $40,000...she was obligated to repay the entire amount within three years!! And, of course, there was no way she could find that kind of money.

I believe the bank president who was involved in the mortgage arrangement felt forever guilty. I knew him until he died. He used to be seen in the winter sitting on the shore, very depressed, because he had contributed to my mother's loss of the theatre. He felt very bad about it because his family was close to ours.

I was only 14 at the time; I don't know any of the details, but that was how she lost the theatre. She tried to hold onto it by running show trains which were theatre excursions. People would come from Minneapolis, Green Bay, or Milwaukee to Chicago for a weekend, during which time they saw three shows, and mother would arrange for them to meet the actors afterwards backstage. The schedule was always one serious play and two light shows because she wanted to educate the theatre audience. I remember seeing Eugene O'Neill's *Long Day's Journey Into Night*, one of the serious dramas. The show trains ran for several years in the fall and winter and were beginning to show some profit. My father, Rodion, helped with this venture plus some Chicago neighbors and an employee in Milwaukee. However, then my mother had bad luck with one of the Milwaukee employees who embezzled $7,000, but she couldn't bear to take him to court because he had a wife and family and a mortgage to pay.

My mother was really falling apart at this point. Haunted by the specter of the impending loss of the theatre, the show trains were a desperate attempt to save the theatre. When this trusted employee stole from her, she just disintegrated. It was such a blow to her. Earlier, when the three-year mortgage was first signed, she'd fallen apart emotionally but then had pulled herself together enough to try to find a solution to save the theatre. She was under tremendous stress and she abused alcohol and pills during these years. It was a horrible situation, and I'm not sure how all of us three kids survived. My mother always had this vision of the theatre and we also shared her dream. We all loved the Players and we still do. In the years before 1959 it was a very special theatre, and the play selection and acting were extraordinarily fine. In 1959 I started college at Columbia University in New York. I had always assumed that my family's little theatre in Fish Creek couldn't possibly be as good as Broadway. I mean, just the name "Broadway" implies excellence. However, when I moved to New York I found that Broadway seldom equaled what we did in Fish Creek in a week!

On Memorial Day during that fateful summer of 1959, my mother had been in a serious car accident near our home in Huntington, Long Island. It was before the days of seat belts and my younger sister, Dounia, hit the windshield and required 60 stitches. Fortunately, there was a good plastic surgeon on duty and she healed with no visible facial scars. My mother had already hired Joseph Papp to be the director that summer but she was hospitalized in serious condition. Because she believed she was unable to open the theatre that summer, she let him and the whole company go. Then, two weeks later, when she was feeling much better, she changed her mind and she and I and my nine- year-old brother Rodion flew to Chicago to find whatever actors were left and hire them. However, in Chicago she ended up in the hospital again with a condition called bronchiectasis, and that summer she had part of her lung removed. She had had this disease for a while, I remember a few years before we had spent several months in the Austrian Alps where the mountain air was supposed to benefit her lungs.

On about June 20, she couldn't bear the thought that the theatre would not be open that summer so she handed me her clipboard and said,

"Héloise, please open it!"

I was just 17 years old and shy whereas she had been an outgoing 19-year-old when she started the theatre. However, it simply didn't occur to her that asking me to do it was too much to ask, and I didn't think I had the option of saying "No". So I agreed to take over and she suggested a few people for me to call. I had been raised in the theatre and by the time I was eight I realized it was more fun to hang out with the grown-ups, so I had years of experience painting scenery, ushering, playbill handouts, and minor walk-on roles. Trying to fill my mother's shoes, however, was overwhelming! While in Chicago we found a few actors who didn't have jobs so our first play was *Champagne Complex* because we had performed it a few years previous and it required only three actors.

My brother Rodion and I rode up to Door County on a Greyhound bus with a Chicago attorney whom my mother had hired to help untangle the situation with the board of directors. Obviously he was a public interest lawyer; otherwise, why else would he be taking a bus to Fish Creek! Meanwhile, my sister Dounia was still in the East with my father, recovering from the car accident.

I went to the theatre to open up all the buildings but we had no water, no electricity, and no car. I had a high school friend from Ephraim who brought over some groceries. Rodion and I cooked hot dogs on the beach; we sunk the milk in buckets in the bay so it wouldn't spoil. We began to go through the buildings and clean them up. One day, Armand, our dog, came running across the beach, which meant that our father had arrived from the East. My first thought was "now we have a car, we can really move." My father brought Roger Hamilton who had helped in the office the previous summer, and he was a great support to me. Meanwhile, my father began discussions with Tom Koutsoukas, the director, about play selection. What did I know about choosing plays?! I was having trouble taking charge, of course. I was only 17 and shy. But, in addition to that, there were certain people whom my mother had always taken care of who landed on me that summer. There was Michael Gnesin, Dr. Gnesin's son, who spent much of the time in a mental hospital but was let out in the summer for vacation. And then his mother, with the improbable name of "Canary", who was widowed and fairly dotty, spent summers at the Players, so I had to deal with both of them. Every day not only did I have to figure out how to keep the whole theatre running but I had to think of tasks to keep them busy so they wouldn't make more trouble for me.

My mother had the actress Hilda Simms come to do Blanche in *Streetcar Named Desire* that summer. She had starred on Broadway but it was many years since she had worked. She had always wanted to do Blanche in *Streetcar* but she had never acted in summer stock before and she was terrified! She was also an alcoholic and an emotional wreck and somehow my mother had sicced her on me. Because she was terrified of having only one week of rehearsal time, she arrived with all her lines memorized. However, because of her drinking, she had forgotten them all by the third day!

On opening night, the Chicago drama critic Sydney Harris, Maggy Magerstadt and I were sitting in the back of the theatre. I was also ushering that night and about 8 p.m. someone came to tell me that part of the scenery had fallen down. I'm wearing a ball gown because in those days all the ushers were dressed in formals, so I went back stage to hammer on the scenery until it was upright again. Then I returned to the back row where we were watching the play and Hilda's performance when Sydney Harris suddenly exclaimed, "Oh my God, she isn't playing Blanche, *she is Blanche*!"

The week was just awful, I couldn't believe it! We had the usual opening night party at Madeline Tourtelot's. As the week progressed, the production never got any better. There was no way it could get better with an alcoholic Blanche.

When the show was finished, I had hoped Hilda would return to New York but she didn't. Instead, she and Michael Gnesin formed a duo and went out drinking every night to bars all over the county. During the day I was getting calls saying, "Can't you stop them...they're driving wildly!" Hilda's décolleté was hanging out all over the place but there was nothing I could do about their behavior short of asking them to leave Door County. But I didn't have that kind of forceful personality, not at 17.

Then there was Joy Walker White, a Texas woman with a lot of money who, for years, had been badgering my mother to perform a play she had written called *A Nest for the Phoenix*. Joy said, "I will underwrite every expense; if this play loses money, I will make up the difference!" My mother called me up and said, "Do it!" She knew the play was a dud because the characters didn't hold together. Jeanne Bolan who was a very good actress had found the lines very difficult to memorize because they didn't relate to the character. We flew in the scenic designer, Kurt Lundell, at great expense.

On opening night, which was also the celebration of the Player's 25th anniversary, without telling me, Joy had paid to have a private ambulance drive my mother from the Chicago hospital to the show. Suddenly, my mother walked slowly down the stairs, so debilitated from her recent surgery that she was unable to sit through the performance. It was the most God-awful scene, I mean it was wrenching. Because she couldn't sit in the theatre she went over to lie down in Mama's house until the play was over, then was whisked back to Chicago to the hospital. It was totally bizarre: she just had major surgery a few weeks before and didn't need to be riding around in an ambulance for hundreds of miles. It was truly appalling—in fact, it was theatre in itself!!

That fateful summer my sister Dounia was just fifteen but helped paint scenery and distribute handbills. My father Rodion was trying desperately to provide financial support. Although his position as a navigator for TWA sounds like a fancy job, his salary in 1959 was only $12,000 a year, and there were a lot of medical bills. He loved my mother dearly and was struggling to drive back and forth to Chicago to visit her in the hospital all summer. I did my best to care for my nine year old brother Rodion Jr. that summer, but he was sort of an abandoned child. I remember Rodion would gather up his own laundry, stumble up the hill to the Buchbinders and ask "Can someone please wash my clothes?" I used to make him take a bath once a week, but otherwise he was largely on his own. Besides visiting my mother, my father would spend some time with Rodion, and time with the director to discuss the plays. So, by some miracle, we got through that summer, opening on the 4th of July weekend as usual and presenting ten plays including such favorites as *Gigi, Blithe Spirit, Bus Stop* and *Born Yesterday*. The show must go on!

The following summer my mother returned to the Players but she had no money and was too debilitated to run the theatre, which was then bankrupt. After that final season, she left and never set foot on the property again! In 1960, Kenneth Carroad, a New York attorney whose wife was my mother's friend, bought the property at a bank sale. At my mother's suggestion, he hired Jim McKenzie to run the theatre. Jim had been associated with the Players since 1947, first as an apprentice but later in various capacities. He followed my mother's philosophy of play selection, which was that nine of the ten plays have to be for the audience, that kind of well done but fun froth, and then you did one serious play for the actors. Through the years, Jim continued in that vein that you did something challenging, something interesting. You simply didn't revisit the golden oldies. He was a risk-taker, willing to try new plays and if they flopped he'd say, "Well, that was not a good one!"

Because of his good theatre management over a forty-year period, the theatre is in wonderful financial shape today!

There are many legends surrounding the Fishers, that brilliant and eccentric family who founded the Players in 1935. Mama Fisher (Lydia) came to America at the age of 13 with her older sister from Silesia in the early 1900's. She graduated from Pratt Institute with a degree in costume design. She was a fine seamstress who not only sewed elaborate costumes for the Players but also made new outfits for Dounia and me every Christmas and on our birthdays. This constituted a major part of our wardrobes because we were living very close to the edge. Apparently she met her husband C.R. Fisher ("Papa") at Palisades Amusement Park in New Jersey. I saw Mama and Papa mainly in the summers at Fish Creek where she not only sewed costumes but also supervised the kitchen. Even when there was a hired cook she was always watching over them. She helped plan the menus and made sure that on opening nights a fruit salad would be served so that the actors' nervous stomachs would not have to cope with a heavy meal. We'd stand in line to get our plates filled and she would dole out the portions to each actor:

"No, you're too heavy, you get only a small portion!" whereas for a skinny person, she'd pile on the food.

In the 1950's, Mama and Papa were living in Hollywood but they'd come for a long summer at the Players. They'd stop in Chicago to pick up our dog, Armand, (we were all still in school) then they'd proceed up to Door County. That's where Mama liked to be; she liked to prepare the theatre gardens along with Edith Dunn. As a child I could wander into the kitchen or into the sewing room to visit with her although she was not someone who invited children's confidences. I remember once she got angry at my brother Rodion—she was somewhat overweight at this point—and she went waddling after him with a toilet plunger in her hand! She had a temper and, at times, yelled and screamed. However, she loved people. Both my grandparents and my mother were very egalitarian. Everyone at the theatre colony was treated equally; the cooks and the babysitters weren't treated any differently than "the stars." That is to say, some actors were "stars" on the handbills but within the theatre community where we all lived together everyone was respected equally.

One thing that was very special about Mama and Papa Fisher was that in the early years they supported Caroline and Richard's dream to start a theatre. Unlike many parents, they didn't say, "Why don't you go out and get a real job and earn a real income!" Almost everyone at the theatre called them "Mama" and "Papa" and it wasn't until I was about thirty years old that I realized that all these people had their own mothers and fathers, sisters and brothers someplace else. The Players was like a family, and I think many of the actors adopted my grandparents as their family because their own families did not accept their career choice. In 1963, Mama Fisher died of pancreatic cancer when she was in her early seventies. I loved her dearly.

Papa Fisher, born Charles Richard Fisher, came from an old Boston whaling family of some wealth who summered in Bar Harbor, Maine. At age twelve he ran away from home and was disowned. He worked in a yard goods store to support himself and managed to put himself through MIT where he received degrees in both civil and electrical engineering. During my mother's early childhood, her parents lived in Rogers City, Michigan on Lake Huron, where Papa had invented the endless conveyor belt for unloading the huge ore boats that plied the Great Lakes. My mother was born in New York City on May 3, 1914, and she spoke German to her mother at home until she entered school. Her brother Richard was born in 1917, and Margo in 1920. The family moved to Chicago where C. R. Fisher was involved in the construction of the outer Lake Shore Drive. He earned a huge amount of money in his lifetime. Apparently, at one point, he earned $100,000 a year and was spending all of it.

When my mother was a teenager, it was her job to do his books and try to insure that some of that money was left over for household expenses. He was a great womanizer and spent his money on wine, women and song! This was very painful for the family. Mother told me that she used to spend every New Year's Eve crying with her mother because it was her mother's birthday and Papa was out with some other woman. My grandparents never divorced but my grandmother was forever furious about her husband's frequent lapses.

One of the funny stories was that he had been visiting one of Al Capone's nightclubs in Chicago where he saw Jean Leslie who was dancing there. He noticed that between shows she was sitting off to one side reading Shakespeare. He befriended her and invited her to come to Fish Creek to perform with the Players. There was never a question of any impropriety between them but Mama and Richard just assumed that Jean was another one of his girlfriends and they barely spoke to her that summer! Jean herself told me this story. An exceptionally talented actress and dancer, she became almost a fixture at the Players, appearing almost every summer from 1947 to 1960. She also became one of my mother's dearest friends; she was like an aunt to me and her children were like my cousins.

Papa was definitely an eccentric and very bright. After Mama died in 1963, he spent time traveling around the country, visiting those old girlfriends, I think. He was very peripatetic, you never knew when he was going to turn up. He never wanted to be pinned down as to an exact arrival date. I remember when I had an apartment on 113th street near Columbia University, and he just appeared at my doorstep one day. As was customary, he announced his arrival with a loud seagull squawk. It was deafening and certainly got your attention. Once he had arrived, he'd stay for 2 or 3 months. We were a bunch of students in our twenties and he was in his seventies then.

He never wanted to dress up which I suppose was some rebellion against his very proper and wealthy background. He seldom shaved and always looked like some kind of wreck. I remember a period when I was dating a man who was later to become my husband. It was Thanksgiving, and I was cooking my first turkey, and his parents, who had been East Coast academics for generations, were coming to dinner. It was my big day but I had never cooked a turkey or baked pies before, and I was cooking on a stove that had no reliable temperature controls. Papa was invited too, but I wondered if he would actually show up at my boyfriend's lower East side apartment. But, miracle of miracles, he arrived all spiffed up in a Chesterfield jacket with velvet collar, and with a bottle of wine for us, but beer for himself. He was absolutely charming and regaled us that afternoon with his stories of wine, women and song. It was wonderful!

When I was twelve I visited my grandfather's boyhood home in Boston when his two elderly sisters were selling the house and moving to Florida. At that time they wanted to give some of the family furniture to my parents. Years later when they died they left some money to Papa's children: Caroline, Richard and Margie. My mother quickly went through her share because she had the philosophy that "money is like manure, it should be spread around so it could do some good." My brother, Rodion, used his share to pay for his medical school education so that portion, at least, was put to good use!

My other grandfather was Basil Rathbone of Sherlock Holmes fame. Born in England in 1892, he received excellent training as a member of his cousin Sir Frank Benson's Shakespearean Company. It was there he met my grandmother, Marion Foreman, who was also a fine actress. They were married in 1914 and my father Rodion was born the following year. It is said that they had been reading Dostoyevsky's *Crime and Punishment* at the time, and named their son for the novel's main character, Rodion

Roskolnikov. Nevertheless, Basil left his wife when Rodion was about three and never saw him again until he was twenty-two. Basil came to America for a great career both on stage and in movies starring Katherine Cornell, Greta Garbo, Eva Le Gallienne, Norma Shearer, John Barrymore, Olivia de Havilland, Errol Flynn and many others.

In 1923 he met Ouida Bergère, a successful screen-writer and theatrical agent, and after he obtained a divorce from Marion Rathbone in 1926, they were married. Ouida and Basil were living in Hollywood in 1937 when Basil encouraged Rodion to come to America, saying maybe he could do something for him in the film industry. My father appeared in two films with Basil: *Dawn Patrol* and *Towers of London*. At the time he met my mother, who was a MGM starlet, he was working as a film editor in the cutting room. A whirlwind courtship ensued and they were married within six weeks.

One of the stories my parents told was that when they returned from the honeymoon, Ouida had found a little apartment for them and had it completely decorated in her own tastes. My parents were very upset because they had looked forward to setting up their own household and furnishing it themselves.

Ouida had very extravagant tastes and another incident occurred in the late 1930's when my parents still lived in Hollywood. Ouida had given a huge party—this was right in the middle of the Depression. Afterwards, it was reported in the Los Angeles newspaper gossip columns that she had spent $150,000 on this party. My father was present when she read the article, which made her absolutely furious,

"How can they write this nonsense??...It wasn't $150,000...I only spent $100,000!!"

Neither of my parents cared much for Hollywood and left a year or so later. During my childhood, my parents never bad-mouthed Ouida but I could tell by the tone of their voice that they didn't like her because over the years she made it very difficult for Rodion to have any relationship with his father. During my childhood we lived in the vicinity of New York where Basil and Ouida had an apartment on Central Park West. My father kept trying to initiate a relationship with his father: he'd write him a letter, he'd telephone him, he'd stop by, he'd spend a night there on his way to Wisconsin in the summer. It was frequently necessary that, in order to see his father, he'd have to go through Ouida. She controlled access.

Up until the time when I went to New York to attend Columbia University, I had never met our famous grandfather. In September 1959, he was appearing on Broadway in a production of Archibald MacLeish's play *J.B.* One night, five girls from my dormitory were planning to see the play so I decided to join them. After the play, I went backstage and told the stage manager that I would like to see Basil Rathbone. They asked me who I was and I replied "I'm his granddaughter!" So I was quickly ushered backstage. I met him for maybe five minutes. He was very cordial and warm. The show was closing in New York and would be going on tour. He would be taking over Christopher Plummer's role of Mr. Nickles (the Devil) instead of playing Mr. Zuss (Job). He said he was very busy—rehearsing during the day and performing at night—however, when he returned in April he said we must have dinner together. Of course I could understand how busy he was because I had just finished running the Peninsula Players for my mother that summer. He did write me several letters over the next few months...I wish I had saved them.

In the meantime both my sister Dounia and I were coming in contact with theatre people who would ask,

"Are you related to Basil Rathbone?"

Every one of them, after just a few minutes of conversation, would then add,

"Oh, Ouida is so awful!!"

This happened at least ten or twelve times, and these comments were completely unsolicited by me, I hadn't even met the woman.

However, I never saw my grandfather again. I made various attempts to contact him but was always put off by Ouida.

My view of Basil, because everyone found him agreeable and enjoyed his company, was he must have been one of those people who are charming to whomever is in front of him at the moment but was unable to make a commitment. He made only one commitment in his life, and that was to Ouida. When it became apparent that I would not be able to see my grandfather, I threw his letters away.

In the early 1960's, my sister Dounia was acting on Broadway in Jerome Robbins "Ballet Ballads" and later in Bob Fosse's "Little Me". She was a versatile and dramatic dancer, just breathtaking to watch. However, she was beginning to feel quite embarrassed that she had never met her famous grandfather, so she too started to make attempts to see him and found out she always had to go through Ouida.

At the time, Ouida was writing her memoirs and Dounia had to sit for hours on end listening to Ouida read from her unfinished autobiography which, at that point, was already over 300 pages. It consisted mainly of list after list of her parties and which famous people had attended. In other words, she was "a name dropper". As far as I know her autobiography was never published. And finally, after three such long afternoons, she allowed Dounia to meet Basil for twenty minutes. And that was the only time that my sister met her grandfather. Ouida controlled everything.

Some years after Basil Rathbone's autobiography *In and Out of Character* was published, I was present when my father received a letter from Basil that said,

"I know I've made many mistakes in my life but I don't ever want to see you again!"

My grandfather died in 1967 at the age of 75. At the time many people felt that he died prematurely because he had to keep working to pay the bills, despite the fact that he was getting older and more tired. He had a one-man show called "An Evening with Basil Rathbone" and in his autobiography he describes traveling to various colleges and universities throughout the country between October and April. In the will my father received a $500 bequest from his father. It was said that in naming some token amount rather than leaving him out altogether, Basil made it more difficult for my father to contest the will. But, of course, my father had no intention of contesting the will. By that time my grandfather no longer had a lot of money because Ouida had spent most of it.

When my grandfather died, my father was in Saudi Arabia flying for TWA. However, my mother felt it was important that someone from our family attend the funeral, so I went with my brother Rodion, Jr. The ushers seated us in the row behind Ouida. After all, we were family but Ouida didn't have a clue who we were. It was at the reception after the service when I met their daughter, Cynthia, for the first time. She was about my age and had been adopted as an infant in 1939 when Ouida was 53 and Basil 47. She seemed very happy to meet my brother and me and, consequently, we met several times over the next few years. It was during one of these visits that she told me the following story:

Several months after her father died, the British government filed a claim against the estate, but, of course, by that time there wasn't much money left. Originally, Basil Rathbone had been paying alimony to his first wife, Marion Foreman Rathbone, with the proviso that if she ever set foot in the United States these payments would cease. In 1947 after the war, she came to the States to visit my parents and her grandchildren with the result that Basil stopped sending her money. At the time she was close to sixty, unable to find work in the theatre, so she applied for the dole. This was during a period when Basil had made sixteen very successful Sherlock Holmes films in addition to two hundred weekly radio broadcasts of the popular detective series for which he had probably earned several million dollars. In any event, Cynthia told me that a few months after her father died, there was a long distance call from Marion Foreman Rathbone and a heated argument ensued between Ouida and Marion as to *who was the real Mrs. Basil Rathbone!!* Both women were close to eighty then.

The only time Cynthia could invite me to their apartment was once when her mother was in the hospital. Cynthia joked that, of course, Ouida couldn't abide the hospital food and was ordering dinner from the 21 Club and Sardi's! I sensed that Cynthia was going through an emotionally difficult time after her father's death because she was much closer to him than to her mother. The last time I saw Cynthia was when she had just been in a hospital and looked terrible. She had some kind of Vitamin K deficiency and her skin was full of blotches. I didn't realize how seriously ill she was, and she died a few months later. Ouida Bergère Rathbone outlived everyone and died in 1974 at the age of eighty-eight. It was said that her real name had been Ida Berger from Brooklyn where she began her career in vaudeville.

Marion Foreman Rathbone was a wonderful character! She certainly wasn't the cuddly type of grandmother nor was she a cuddly sort of mom to my father, Rodion, because she was completely focused on herself and her career. She was the grande dame of Shakespearean theatre in England, and she and Basil had been members of the Frank Benson Company when they married. After their divorce in 1926 it was difficult for her to find work because in those days a divorced woman was a pariah! So she continued to do whatever she could to earn money by giving readings and lectures but she never worked at that same level again.

When I was 14 or 15, Marion lived with us for two summers and one winter in 1956-57. She wanted to be the grande dame at the Players, but instead she was helping out at the gift shop and not very happy. However, all you had to say was "Marion, would you do a scene for us?" and she'd be up on that stage in a minute! She knew five Shakespeare plays in their entirety and scenes from all of the others. Even in the summer, she wore a short black cape, and she had a longer over cape too, so she was always ready to perform. It was her costume. She used different voices for different characters; she played all the roles—*and she was stunning*!! I get goosebumps even thinking about those performances. I remember one evening at one of Maggy Magerstadt Rosner's cocktail parties where Marion performed the courtroom scene from the *Merchant of Venice* under one of the trees. In the Shylock speech, her voice just boomed! It was so powerful that when she finished, everyone was just stunned into silence. A year later, in my high school English class, my teacher assigned me the role of Shylock. A part of Marion's interpretation must have still resonated within me because after I finished reading Shylock's speech, the classroom fell quiet. Because of Marion, I had absorbed that speech—I had heard it and understood it in a way that I never would have otherwise. Marion's talent was so exceptional, it made you realize that those performances with the Frank Benson Company (which later became the Stratford Festival Company) must have been extraordinary!

So my father, Rodion, grew up in fine theatre and my mother, Caroline, was creating fine theatre. In those early days of the Peninsula Players, the actors who performed there did not come for the money: they were being paid $25 a week plus room and board to be "stars". Actors Equity allowed that theatre to have a lower pay scale because, otherwise, they knew it would die. Nowadays, Door County is very different from the early days when there wasn't much of a tourist crowd nor was it an artistic tourist crowd. My mother founded the theatre in 1935, I believe the same year that Jens Jensen began The Clearing.

When I was first married in 1968, as part of our honeymoon, my husband and I drove around England where we visited Marion and I met her three sisters, Millie, Lillian and Gwen for the first time. Of that family, Marion was the actress, Lillian and Gwen had been dancers in their youth, and Millie was Britain's first female certified public accountant. Lillian and her husband, Tom, then living in Devon, were such dear people and must have provided the real warmth for my father when he was a child growing up in Wales. When I visited Marion in Newport she was completely focused on herself as usual. Her walls were covered with her theatre history and that had been the center of her life—she never paid much attention to anyone else. In her later career she had assisted in Shakespeare productions in various Welsh castles in Caerphilly, Chepstor and Usk. When she was in her eighties, she had a fall and could no longer live on her own. My father found a retired actors home in London where she received good care and she died there in the early 1970's.

My parents viewed travel as an adventure and in 1947, when my father was with The Royal Canadian Air Force, we lived in Rome for nine months. My mother did war relief work in Naples with homeless families living in caves and I remember she came home with lice. We lived in Austria for several months in 1951, and in 1960 we spent time in Portugal.

Their most exotic sojourn, however, was the ten years they lived in Saudi Arabia, where my father worked for TWA from 1967-77. The Saudis were setting up a national airline, Saud Air, and my father instructed young pilots in the mechanics and engineering of the aircraft they were learning to fly. In Arabia, my parents had an active social life with both Westerners and Saudis, complicated however by the prevailing sleep customs. In those days telephones were not common so Arab friends might turn up at your doorstep at ten at night, having taken a siesta in the heat of the day. In the evening the temperature might be only 100°F so it made sense to socialize at night. My parents were living in an eight story building originally constructed by the mayor of Jiddah to house his family, his sons and various wives in different apartments.

Occasionally, my father was the navigator on Saud Air when the Royal Family went abroad, usually for medical treatment. Another time, King Faisal and his entourage took a round-the-world trip across the Pacific and their final destination was Washington D.C. where they met with President Nixon. My father told me that at every stop along the way, the crew would be handed $500 to spend for entertainment. When he reached San Francisco, he telephoned me and said, "Please come to Washington D.C. next weekend…I want you to experience some of this!"

So he put my husband and myself in the same hotel with King Faisal's entourage. At that time, there was also a convention going on of creative anachronists whose members were dressed in medieval costumes pretending to be royalty and nobility while participating in jousts and banquets. It was such a strange juxtaposition of, on the one hand, people dressed like medieval kings and queens—and on the other, the real-life anachronism of King Faisal from Arabia whose kingdom, at least in the late 1960's, was still in many ways medieval!

I remember when I visited my parents in Saudi Arabia in 1968 and my mother, my brother's girlfriend and I were invited to the marriage celebration of the mayor of Jiddah's daughter which took place in their villa across the street. The party began at 11 p.m. when it was cooler, and was held in the villa garden, which was furnished with plush Persian carpets and comfortable chairs. This was a ladies party because it was customary for the sexes to be separated at weddings, and one third of the women were veiled. Therefore, I was surprised to see a group of male entertainers dancing on stage. When I asked who they were, I was told, "Oh, they're eunuchs!"

And I remember thinking to myself, "Where am I, what century am I in?" The party went on until daylight.

Having grown up in a family where money was scarce, my father Rodion was determined to be a better father than his own father had been…and, indeed, he was. His other objective was to support his family financially, in as much as his own father had not. These were his two main goals in life, and he succeeded in both of them. When he was elderly, he developed Alzheimer's disease and came to live with me for five years in Brooklyn. Because I was working I had a home health aide who would come in during the day, but then he began to wander not only during the day but also at night. Once he walked several miles to the Brooklyn Bridge where some actors found him, realized he was confused, and kindly brought him home. He would set out three or four times a day, trying to walk to Darien, Connecticut where he last lived and where he had a favorite bank manager. By that time he had forgotten that you could take a train to Darien. Eventually, I realized I could no longer care for him so he spent his final years in a nursing home where he died in 1996 at the age of 81.

Leo Lucker, a founding member of the Peninsula Players, acted and directed there for 25 years, and he remained a close friend of my family; he was also my godfather. He was a dear, lovely man who in his final years had suffered from ulcers, several strokes and a heart attack. He loved the opera, and for years Marianna Collins, who was Oscar Mayer's granddaughter, had bought him sixth row center season tickets to the Metropolitan Opera. At the time he was living at my mother's apartment, where she had full-time home health aides taking care of him.

In February 1977 we went to see *Magic Flute* together. He was so looking forward to it; his caretaker told me he had gotten up at 3 a.m. that morning to get ready. By then he had lost his sense of time. We went by cab and as he watched the opera he became aware that he didn't know what scene was coming next—an opera which he had enjoyed so many times before.

I didn't realize it then but that night he made the decision that he didn't want to continue living. If his mind was that far gone that he couldn't remember scenes from *Magic Flute*, it was time to end it. That was on Tuesday night. He spent the next few days getting his papers in order—he couldn't write any more but he made little stacks of his papers. Then he asked the home health aide to take him to the bank to take out some passbooks.

On Friday he went to my mother, gave her some Christmas cards, told her how much he loved her and basically said "goodbye" to her. Then for the next few days he refused all food and water. I visited him Monday at the VA Hospital and he could barely speak. I wished I had stayed just a little longer because he died twenty minutes after I left.

When my mother was sixty-seven, she was diagnosed with Charcot-Marie-Tooth disease which is a type of peripheral neuropathy and muscle atrophy similar to Lou Gerhig's disease. During my mother's final years, my parents were living in Norwalk, Connecticut in a peaceful country place with wooded acreage. Often on weekends, old theatre friends from the Players would come out from New York for a visit—Maggy Magerstadt Rosner, Jim McKenzie, Jean Sincere, Maurice Ottinger, and Bill Russell. My mother had been an inspired cook and still managed to do so in her wheelchair. Her last two years she was bedridden and my father took care of her with some help from us children on weekends. She died on May 2, 1985, one day short of her 71st birthday.

And now, my vibrant parents and grandparents are all gone—just ghosts whose dreams and dramas, illusions and eccentricities once haunted my childhood years. Yet, my mother's vision of creating theatre has endured; and the Peninsula Players continues to weave its web of enchantment!

Héloise Rathbone
New York City
March 2003

Chapter 13
Peninsula Players Revisited:
1976 to Present

In Spring of 1976, I had just returned from my second encounter with Broadway, that "fickle mistress," after the brief run of *Angel Street* starring Dina Merrill, when Jim McKenzie called asking me to return to the Players that summer as artistic director. His wife Jeanne Bolan, an accomplished and versatile actress and the mother of Kevin, David and Amy, had died that March of cancer. For the previous fifteen years she had been the Player's leading lady and artistic director. She was only 49.

Margaret and I had recently purchased a 22-foot Winnebago motor home which we nicknamed "Winnie" so we drove to Door County that summer and parked it at Camp-Tel in Egg Harbor. Because of increased tourism, the Players had adopted a saner schedule of presenting only five plays a season, each running two weeks, instead of the earlier killer pace of ten plays. Under Actors' Equity, our rehearsal hours also became tidier. A typical day consisted of a three-hour morning rehearsal starting at ten, a lunch break, and then a two-hour afternoon rehearsal followed by dinner and the evening performance.

Tom Birmingham, former Gibraltar School Superintendent, later with the University of Wisconsin-Green Bay, and the father of eleven wonderful kids, became the Player's general manager that year. Between Tom, Jim McKenzie and I we formed a triumvirate, working closely together to choose the plays for each new season. The driving force, however, behind the Players' growing success over a forty year period was Jim McKenzie, who was not only a visionary but also possessed formidable organizational skills. In the early years, the theatre was not a money-making operation, but Jim and his family worked very hard to build the full houses that we enjoy today. Because he was based near New York and also later in San Francisco, he had his finger on Broadway's pulse: he saw all the new plays, he knew the playwrights, he made the right connections. For example, in 1955 there was an apprentice at the Players named Emanuel Linton. Twenty years later that same man whose real name was Emanuel Azenburg was now Neil Simon's theatrical agent and consequently, Jim McKenzie and this little provincial theatre in Fish Creek, Wisconsin could obtain the production rights to Simon's latest hits: *Plaza Suite, Brighton Beach Memoirs, God's Favorite, The Odd Couple, Barefoot in the Park* and others, before major cities could, and often while they were still in their Broadway run!

Every spring, Jim, Tom and I would mull over play selection, with Tom and I favoring more traditional shows—the old classics, some thrillers, amusing comedies—whereas Jim would argue for the avant-garde. Our discussions became quite heated at times, but in the end we compromised and found a good balance. Actors' auditions took place in Chicago in the spring, where we hired actors who were suitable for roles in a number of plays.

Equus, in the 1977 season, was a powerful and controversial play about a disturbed stable boy who blinded horses. When I was doing *Angel Street* on Broadway the previous year, I ran into Tony Perkins who was starring in *Equus* in a theatre just a few doors away. He had just replaced Richard Burton in the role, and he told me that he found the play very depressing. (This, from the actor who played the deranged murderer in "Psycho"!) In *Equus* he was the psychiatrist, Dr. Dysart, (the same role I played in the Fish Creek production) and there were pages of psychiatric monologues to be memorized. However, the Fish Creek audiences loved the play even though we eliminated the nude lady on horseback, thinking it would be too risqué. In those days we had to be quite decorous in the language used onstage; we didn't want to offend any conservative sensibilities—although crude language seems to be the norm on television today. What passes for dialogue often seems to be just a steady stream of profanity, topped off with a frisson of "f" words!

In that first 1976 season I directed two plays which I had recently acted in at the Candlelight-Forum Theatre in Chicago: *God's Favorite* by Neil Simon, where I played Job in both productions, and *Solitaire, Double Solitaire* by Robert Anderson. In early September our oldest son, David, was being married in California, so Margaret and I had to leave before *Solitaire* was finished.

That fall I had been invited to join the venerable Alley Theatre in Houston, Texas, as part of their resident company, so Margaret and I had an enjoyable trip to Texas in our motor home. The theatre, founded in 1946 by Nina Vance, was known for its brilliant productions of avant-garde work plus solid classics. Plays by David Mamet, George Bernard Shaw, Pirandello, Pavel Kohout (Czech), Lillian Hellman, Paul Zindel, Mikhail Roschin (Russian), Oscar Wilde, Athol Fugard (South African), and Alan Ayckbourne had been performed in recent years in addition to a cooperative venture with Moscow's Sovremennik Theatre.

The Alley Theatre was in downtown Houston across from the Opera House, and nearby was a large cancer treatment hospital where it was common for patients who needed several months of treatment to come in their motor homes. Therefore, the hospital had provided a large parking area complete with hook-ups and a security fence, and it was there that Margaret and I spent the winter of 1976, from October until April. I could walk to the theatre, we had escaped the Chicago winter, and it was cheap! During our six month stay, I appeared in three plays: Old Crompton in *You Never Can Tell* by George Bernard Shaw; the Squire in

The Corn is Green by Emlyn Williams, and a monsignor in *The Runner Stumbles.*

In 1978, the Players did *The Shadow Box*, by Michael Cristofer, a play about several terminal cancer patients and an elderly woman in a wheelchair. Over the years, Jim McKenzie often visited Caroline Rathbone in Connecticut and thought she might play the part. When she contacted me about the role, she sounded enthusiastic over the phone—it was the first time we had spoken in over twenty years. Tom Birmingham and I assured her that we would double cast the role in the event she didn't feel up to it, so we cast the actress Marji Bank, just in case. One week before rehearsals began, Caroline called to say,

"Bob, I just can't do it...I'm going to have to back out. I can't come. It's foolish...I'm in a wheelchair and how could I get around??"

It was very sad. I knew she wanted to come to the Players one last time...to her theatre, to the dream she had given birth to, nourished, and eventually lost. But it was not to be.

Over the years, I have been very fortunate to have played opposite the fine actress Jean Sincere, who has often been my wife on stage. There was an energy about Jean, an edge, and sparks of both anger and tenderness flew between us—just like a real married couple. We acted together in some of my very favorite plays: *Da* in 1979, that powerful Irish play by Hugh Leonard about a son who has returned for his father's funeral, and through a series of flashbacks comes to terms with his ambivalent feelings about his "Da," whom he always viewed as a failure. In the end he comes to recognize his father's ultimate strength and humanity. I loved playing "Da", a fully developed and emotionally complex Irish character. And in 1980, Jean and I played Ethel and Norman Thayer in *On Golden Pond* by Ernest Thompson, set in a Maine lake cabin that the New England couple had visited for the last 48 summers. Norman is an 80-year-old man who is alternately crotchety and irritable about his growing frailty and terrified of death. I was 63 when I played in *On Golden Pond* and its meaning resonates more strongly each year now that I have passed even Norman's age. The playwright's aunt came to see the Fish Creek production and it meant a great deal to me when, afterwards, she came backstage to tell me that, "You're the one the play was written for—you embodied the part!"

Other memorable plays with Jean Sincere were *Foxfire* in 1983, and *Painting Churches* in 1984.

Greg Vinkler and I had played together in *Angel Street* at the Northlight Theatre in Evanston in January 1980 where Greg had played a very sinister Mr. Manningham, intent on driving his wife insane, and I was Sergeant Rough again. I invited Greg to come to Fish Creek that summer to reprise his role in *Angel Street;* however, because of prior commitments, he was unable to, so Michael Tezla played Manningham instead. Finally, in 1988, Greg came to the Players in the production of *Doubles*, and in 1991 he became the theatre's artistic director.

Jim McKenzie, ever the enthusiastic promoter, was associated with the American Conservatory Theatre in San Francisco, where Burt Lancaster and Kirk Douglas were appearing in *The Boys in Autumn*, a play about what happened to Tom Sawyer and Huck Finn once they grew up. He hired them to do the play in Fish Creek that summer. Both Tom Birmingham and I were wildly skeptical as to whether it would actually come to pass that these two Hollywood mega-stars would turn up in little Fish Creek, Wisconsin, so we double cast the play with Dennis Kennedy and Michael Tezla as well. Throughout the rehearsal period we heard rumors that Kirk and Burt were not getting along together in the San Francisco production—that these two macho egos were constantly fighting. In the end they cancelled, and Dennis Kennedy and Michael Tezla had a major success in *Boys in Autumn*.

That same summer I directed Pamela Gay and Pat Walker in *Children of a Lesser God*, a play about the deaf. All of the previous winter, these two dedicated young actors had worked with a deaf person to learn sign language, and that Spring they came to my Downers Grove home to audition for the part. As they read and signed from the script, they were so excellent that I hired them on the spot! It was a memorable production that summer but an especially touching moment came on opening night when, during the curtain call, Pat Walker signed to Pam,

"Will you marry me?"

And her answer, in sign language was,

"Yes!!"

They were married, had two children, and spent eight seasons with the Players. Pat was a fine actor and business manager and they later moved to California.

The theatre colony at Fish Creek has always had its share of zany characters and eccentrics who also happen to be popular actors. Dennis Kennedy, a great audience favorite for twenty years from 1966-86, was cast in all of Neil Simon's plays and most of the Irish plays like *Juno and the Paycock*, *Da* and *A Life*. Dennis enjoyed making people laugh, he loved audience attention, but he also liked to drink and was the toast of every bar in Door County. To quote Maggie Rosner,

"He was the perfect Dublin barfly!"

He was also the weirdest guy in the world. For example, he had assumed the character of an Irish Republican Army rep and an IRA flag was hung at his cabin door. Besides that, he was also a Civil War buff and flew the Confederate flag, too. Upon rising each morning he'd call his troops to attention, salute the Confederate flag and then turn to salute the

Irish flag. He was a manic Chicago Cubs fan and had a radio show called *Denny's Den* where he held forth about the Cubs, the IRA, the Confederate Army and the theatre, roughly in that order, but also including any other subject which caught his fancy. Everyone in Door County knew him and I was frequently asked,

"When is Denny going to be in another show??"

Maggie Rosner tells a wonderful story that took place in the 1960's when John F. Kennedy was still President. At one point, Dennis was obsessed with some question and wanted the Pope's opinion on it. (He had probably had a few drinks too many.) So he telephoned the Vatican from the Players' lodge and said,

"This is Mr. Kennedy calling from America, and he has an important question which requires the Pope's opinion!"

Several hours later, long after Dennis had forgotten about it and driven off to some tavern, I happened to be in the Lodge when the telephone rang and a long distance operator announced,

"Vatican City calling for Mr. Kennedy!"

Dennis had a long career at the Goodman Theatre and acted in several of their "Christmas Carol" productions, in addition to various seasons with the American Conservatory Theatre in San Francisco, the Guthrie Theatre, and the Milwaukee Repertory Theatre!

Carle Benson was another interesting guy who acted at the Players from 1967 to 1989. With a bubble top van filled with golf clubs and other accoutrements that had nothing to do with theatre, he traveled around the country to various acting jobs. He had had seven or eight wives, usually actresses, but when he was between marriages he always had a couple of lady friends stashed away in the wings. In fact, there were few women at the Players whom Carle had not "known", in some way or other. He was always discreetly amorous. In 1977, I acted in *California Suite*, a sophisticated comedy by Neil Simon, with his then wife, Chris Wilson. In the end, however, Carle followed his penchant for Spanish waitresses, and while traveling in Mexico got some kind of leg infection. Either through neglect or poor medical care, by the time he went to a hospital they had to amputate his leg! Nevertheless, he still managed to play golf for another fifteen years. Carle was a versatile repertory actor and his final play at Fish Creek was *A Walk in the Woods* with Greg Vinkler.

Another stalwart performer was the glamorous and elegant Jeannette Leahy who appeared on the Players' stage for twenty-five summers between 1960 and 1993. Besides her work in Fish Creek she had an extensive career in TV, radio and theatre, playing opposite such stars as Phyllis Diller, Ray Milland, Ann Sothern, Louis Nye, Don Ameche, and many others.

The spirited actress Amy McKenzie has literally grown up in the theatre, having inherited talent from both her parents, Jeanne Bolan and James McKenzie. In the 1970's and 1980's, when I was the Players' artistic director, Amy was just developing her actor's craft and I like to believe that I helped influence this process. Amy is a gifted comedienne, very versatile, and over the years has become a talented director herself. She is also lovely to look at and has graced the Players' stage for the past twenty-five years.

The brilliant and witty dialogue of Oscar Wilde's plays has seldom been equaled, and over the years I had been part of several productions of *The Importance of Being Earnest* both at the Goodman Theatre School and at Rosary College. For an actor the role of Lady Bracknell, with its clever repartee satirizing upper-crust British Victorian society, is an especially juicy plum; and in 1985, three months short of my 70th birthday, I was finally going to play this formidable grande dame! Henry Shea, *Door County Advocate*'s veteran reporter, entered completely into the spirit of an elaborate ruse by announcing that,

"The distinguished British character actress, Dame Edwina Mealing, has been hired to play Lady Bracknell and is coming to Door County from her Middlesex, England home especially for the role. Despite the fact that Dame Mealing is descended from a theatrical family which dated all the way back to her 18th century relative, the famous Shakespearean actor David Garrick, she has deigned to travel to this little provincial theatre to appear in this coveted role."

Of course, Edward Mealing Thompson had been the name of my British grandfather so I felt I had a perfect right to take as my stage name, "Edwina Mealing"!

As I began to mentally prepare for the Lady Bracknell character, I envisioned my Aunt Faye Van der Veer, who was herself an outspoken and domineering woman, almost six feet in height, of imposing girth, and much given to the wearing of flamboyant hats. I designed my own costume with ample ruffles and bustles and a mere suggestion of a whalebone corset capable of steadying a battleship on the high seas. Bill Wedepohl, the Players' excellent costume designer since 1972, executed this matronly masterpiece in regal purple and mauve velvet with dignified dove-gray lace at the neckline and wrists topped off with a graceful ostrich plume hat. As I developed the character I imagined how Aunt Faye might walk in such a costume or how, with commanding presence, she might enter a room. The playbill itself showed a photograph of Dame Edwina Mealing wearing a pillbox hat and wig and listed her extensive acting credits. I had a tremendous romp as Lady Bracknell and one critic described Dame Edwina Mealing as,

"A distinguished actress, tall and sturdy, possessing a time worn countenance with a bass voice—the very picture of a haughty aristocrat!"

During one of the performances, there was an annoying contretemps with a bat that was upstaging Lady Bracknell's performance, and it was necessary for me to gather up my skirts and go after the winged marsupial with my parasol. I chased it offstage, which was most unladylike, and as for my splendid gown, it might have been a catastrophe!

Amy McKenzie and Pamela Gay played the roles of Gwendolen Fairfax and Cecily Cardew, and Rich O'Donnell and Michael Tezla played Algernon Moncrieff and Earnest Worthing. Dennis Kennedy was Dr. Chasuble, and Vicki Childers as Miss Prism.

An amusing event, which was a fitting end to that delightful play, occurred during a performance when my wife Margaret was sitting in a back row next to two older matrons. As I came onstage and began to speak, one of the ladies leaned over to her friend and whispered,

"Isn't that Bob Thompson playing Lady Bracknell?"

And her friend replied with some conviction,

"Oh no, he's been dead for years!"

Margaret smiled quietly to herself but said nothing.

Another play which is a zany comedy and a great audience favorite was the 1995 production of *You Can't Take it With You* in which I played Martin Vanderhof, the Sycamore family patriarch who retires from work 35 years early, preferring to spend time at home collecting snakes, attending circuses and graduations, and generally enjoying family life, but neglecting to pay income tax. The Pulitzer Prize winning play by Moss Hart and George Kaufman opened on Broadway in 1936, and the uproarious comedy is still a winner today. The previous winter I had performed the role of Martin Vanderhof at the Candlelight Forum Theatre in Chicago and Chicago Tribune Theatre Critic, Richard Christiansen was kind enough to write,

"Bob Thompson who, at age 78, gives the performance of his career. Rosy cheeked and white-thatched, Thompson is as shrewd a foxy grandpa, as lovable an old codger and as decent a human being as the play's authors could have wished."
Chicago Tribune, December 2, 1994

Since I began at the Players in 1938 I have appeared in close to 100 plays and have directed an additional fifty plays. Despite my age, I'm still having a wonderful time on stage! In 2001, I was offered the opportunity of a lifetime by Tom Mula, who created a play especially for me called *Bob Almighty*, about an elderly man in a wheelchair who thinks he's God. His daughter has placed him in a nursing home and somehow, miracles do seem to happen all around him. In the spring of that year, I had done a reading of the play in Chicago and was very excited about this new project—I thought the play was very good. However, that January I had spent 20 days in the hospital for colon surgery and then we sold our Downers Grove home where I had lived for almost sixty-seven years and moved to Sister Bay, Wisconsin. Between recuperating from major surgery at 84, and the emotional and physical upheaval of packing up and getting rid of the accumulation of several decades of possessions, it was a very stressful time for me. For the first time in my career I was having difficulty memorizing my lines. I counted the lines in *Bob Almighty* and there were 300, and I was simply unable to retain them. So I called Todd Schmidt and Greg Vinkler and told them I was going to have to bow out. The only other time I had to turn down a part was during that Tennessee Williams fiasco years before. Fortunately, the Players were able to hire Howard Witt, a very powerful actor, who came in and did the part on fairly short notice. Nevertheless, he did an excellent job and I enjoyed watching him perform "my role"!

Later that summer I had a small part in *The Cherry Orchard* as the devoted old servant of an aristocratic Russian family that, through fiscal imprudence, has lost its country estate—its beloved cherry orchard is soon to be torn down and replaced with houses. In this play, I have the final scene that's always a boon for an actor because you're able to set the mood for the play's ending. In *Cherry Orchard*, despite a lifetime of loyal servitude, the family members, in their haste to depart, have thoughtlessly left their doddering, frail servant behind. It's a poignant moment and the implication is that he will soon die—penniless and without family.

In 1991, my good friend Tom Birmingham, the theatre's long-time general manager, was ill with a brain tumor. That summer he had hired Todd Schmidt to help with publicity and later Todd assumed Tom's position, often conferring with him by telephone about the theatre's operation, while Tom was in the hospital. Tom died in the spring of 1992 and since that time Todd has become an excellent general manager. He is uniquely qualified for this position, having an undergraduate degree in business, and an MFA degree in directing from the Goodman Theatre School. In other words, Todd is a true Renaissance man, good with people and a very nice guy. And Greg Vinkler took over my role as the Players' artistic director in 1991. Greg has over twenty-five years of acting experience both in Shakespeare repertory and extensive work in Chicago theatres, and we are extremely lucky to have someone of his experience, ability and sensitivity in this important position.

Jim McKenzie, executive producer of the Players, died in the spring of 2002. He began as an apprentice in 1947, and had 56 seasons at the theatre, 40 of them as producer. Through his wise stewardship the tradition of fine theatre in a spectacular natural setting has been nurtured and kept alive. And with Todd Schmidt and Greg Vinkler now at the helm, I have no doubt that the Peninsula Players will continue to create theatre magic for years to come, long after I am gone.

Chapter 14
The World's a Stage

Besides the theatre I have always been possessed with an absolute "wanderlust"—a passion for travel that dates back to my childhood fantasy of becoming a sea captain. In 1966, the good Rosary College nuns granted me a semester sabbatical leave with full pay to study European theatre. We had one son in college, and Margaret's parents had agreed to stay in our home and look after our two high-school age kids, so Margaret and I were free, at last, to do some serious traveling. I am fortunate that my wife shares my curiosity and enthusiasm for travel, and for me half the fun of any trip is the planning involved. I enjoyed working out the itinerary for our ten-week trip; Pan-Am Airlines offered a round-trip ticket with unlimited stopovers for $600, and the travel guide *Europe On $5 a Day* became my bible. On a college professor's salary, Margaret and I could be footloose and fancy free, but not extravagant! Even the kindly Sisters of Rosary were caught up in the vagabond spirit and suggested that, "If you are going to Munich you must stay at this hotel which is run by a religious order, you'll be well treated there!"

Our first stop was Dublin, home of the Abbey Theatre, where my beloved voice and diction teacher from the Goodman, Mary Agnes Doyle, had begun her distinguished career. There we stayed at the Powerscourt Royal Hotel and we spent several days meandering through the Georgian squares along the River Liffey and past Trinity College's soaring Gothic spires and fantastically ornate gates. This was our first visit to Dublin, birthplace of the legendary playwrights: Richard Sheridan, Oscar Wilde, George Bernard

Shaw, Sean O'Casey, Samuel Beckett, and writers: Oliver Goldsmith, James Joyce, William Butler Yeats, John M. Synge, and Brendan Behan. What is it about that city which has fostered such creative brilliance? For me, it was a privilege just to breathe the rarified air of that historic city where, every night, we went out to the theatre.

When we reached London we settled in at the centrally located Georgian Hotel on Marylebone Road near Madame Tussaud's, and from there we explored the city on foot. A highlight was the visit to Wesley Chapel where I mounted the pulpit from which John Wesley, eighteenth century Methodist Church founder, gave his impassioned sermons. Between museum visits we went to the theatre every night—tickets were only $15. Once, when a play was sold out I explained to the box office manager that I was a visiting drama professor and couldn't he just squeeze us in somewhere. "I'll see what I can do," he replied and kindly found us seats for the performance that evening.

Over the years we had kept in contact with Marion Foreman Rathbone through Christmas cards, and as soon as we arrived in London, we telephoned her. She was in her late seventies then and living in Wales but she came by train and we met her at Paddington Station. Together we strolled along Park Lane through Hyde Park towards the West End, and along the way we had a bite to eat at some charming little restaurant. Afterwards, we walked to the theatre district where she glanced up at a marquee and said,

"We must see this play…my friend, Clifford Abbott, is in it and we worked together years ago!"

So we went inside where after effusive hugs and kisses, she introduced us to him. The backstage manager and a few of the technical crew recognized her too, which I'm sure was very gratifying for her. Later that afternoon we put her back on the train to Wales; it had been a memorable day for all of us!

We flew to Amsterdam for three days of more theatre and music at the Concertgebouw (concert hall). One of the plays was *De Dood van de Handelsreiziger*; I had no idea what it was, beforehand, but we bought tickets anyway. The dialogue was in Dutch, of course, but after only a few minutes I realized we were watching *Death of a Salesman* by Arthur Miller. I knew the plot, of course, so it was interesting to hear it performed in another language. Now that I was almost a native, we ventured into a restaurant where the menu was in Dutch and Flemish. When the waiter took our order I more or less just pointed to something that sounded appetizing. When the dish arrived it was quite good but with an unfamiliar taste, so I checked the menu again out of curiosity and realized that "viande de cheval" was horsemeat!

We spent several days in Oslo where we went to an Ibsen play; went on to Copenhagen, where we had dinner with a Danish family with whom the AFS student, Roger Powell from Downers Grove, was living that year. Then we flew from Hamburg to Berlin, where we visited Brandenburger Gate and the Kaiser Wilhelm Gedächtniskirche, and strolled along Kurfürstendamm, the elegant shopping boulevard. Most shocking to us was our East Berlin bus tour, during which we saw old women hunched over broomsticks sweeping streets which were almost empty of cars. Along the Unter den Lindenstrasse, the tired facades of the Reichstag and other municipal buildings were festooned with bright red banners which proclaimed:

"This is the Real Berlin!"

But the contrast with the West was so stark that we were hardly surprised when, as our tour bus paused at the checkpoint to leave the dilapidated buildings and depressing atmosphere behind, the border guards held huge mirrors under our vehicle to make sure no one was escaping to freedom! While in Berlin we saw avant-garde, experimental theatre, and the "pièce de resistance" was the performance of

Maria Callas and Guiseppe di Stefano in a Franz Lehar opera at the Berlin Opera House!

We flew to Cologne and traveled by train to Mannheim to visit Gaby Bolevec, our German AFS student who had lived with us in Downers Grove two years before. Margaret went to the opera with Gaby's mother who spoke no English. Margaret didn't know German, but somehow they communicated and liked each other.

Afterwards we rented a car and drove south along the Rhine, stopping at scenic little restaurants where it was possible to have a delicious meal with a glass of wine for only a dollar. The exchange rate was very good then—four Marks to the dollar. The baroque capital of Bavaria, Munich, is filled with architectural treasures: Nymphenburger Schloss, one of King Ludwig's palaces; the Residenz with its rococco Cuvilliés Theater, the domes of the Frauenkirche in Marienplatz square, the charming Rathaus Glockenspiel. And of course, we heeded the advice of the good nuns at Rosary College, and stayed at the hotel near Hauptbahnhof where we were, indeed, well looked after by the nuns.

The ancestral home of the Habsburgs is Vienna where we stayed five nights at Hotel Graben—in those days a room cost only $5 a night. Years later we returned to Vienna and our same room was $140! The baroque splendor of Schönbrunn Palace, the Vienna Opera, Saint Stefan's Church, and the cozy little pastry shops where we'd stop for afternoon kaffee and kuchen, made Vienna a city we wanted to visit again.

Once you become part of the AFS (American Field Service) foreign exchange student program, you automatically have friends all over the world. In the summer of 1964 our eldest son, David, was an AFS student to Brussels, and when we visited Paris as part of our theatre tour we stayed with the Ferét family, friends of David's Belgian host family. During our four-day visit they taught us to use the Metro so we were quite independent. Glorious Paris, the cultural capital of Europe, whose history goes back to the Romans! Besides the Arc de Triomphe, the Louvre, Notre Dame we explored the quaint shops and sidewalk cafes of Saint-Germain des Près on the Left Bank.

Our final visit was Brussels, where we stayed ten days with the Debekker family, David's Belgian host family. They had had three older children, Denise, Danielle, and a son, Jean-Marie. Their house was not far from Brussels' magnificent main square dominated by ornate buildings of 17th century Flemish Renaissance. Beautiful outdoor flower markets, inviting sidewalk cafes, the Palais Royal, splendid churches and the Musées Royaux des Beaux-Arts with its fine collection of Flemish art and many Dutch masters—the city was lovely and we revisited it in subsequent years. One of the Debekker uncles kindly drove us to visit the medieval jeweled cities of Bruges and Ghent—we were given a complete tour of this fascinating country!

A few days before our return flight to New York we telephoned Sherrill Milnes who, in his youth, had been Margaret's violin pupil. Sherrill met us at JFK Airport and drove us to his home in New Jersey where we stayed for several days. At the time he was singing in *Faust* at the Metropolitan Opera, so he got us tickets. What a fitting end to an unforgettable trip—hearing Sherrill Milnes sing at the Met!

When I returned to Rosary College I had assumed that the nuns expected me to write a learned thesis and give a program on the state of modern European theatre; however, they didn't seem that interested. They were just happy that Margaret and I had had a wonderful trip and that I had gotten a bit of a rest. I did, however, regale my theatre students with tales of our trip for several weeks afterwards.

For much of the 1970's I was working steadily in the theatre, acting and directing in both Chicago and Door County, and with a few brief flings on Broadway. We didn't travel abroad again until April 1979, when we took an eighteen-day tour of England, Scotland and Wales, with an additional visit to the home of my English cousins Alaric and Helen Rowntree, who lived north of London in Hampstead, and had done extensive genealogical research on the Thompson family. One day we went to Brixton, an impoverished area of East London, which, at that time, was notorious for race riots; and there we spent a few hours tromping through a neglected and forgotten cemetery of lichen-etched tombstones hidden in weeds. By lifting up several broken headstones we eventually discovered the one belonging to "Thomas A. Thompson and his wife, Eliza", my great-grandparents who, in Victorian times, lived in Brixton when it was a respectable neighborhood. My great-grandfather worked as a ship's chandler supplying provisions to sailing vessels on the nearby Thames River. In this cemetery, generations of Thompsons lay buried, one on top of each other. My grandfather, Edward Mealing Thompson, was the only member of his family to immigrate to America.

Margaret and I were now in our sixties and seventies and had discovered the convenience of traveling by tour or on a cruise ship. That way I didn't have to make all the hotel arrangements myself, nor schlep suitcases through railroad stations or airports. All that was necessary was to pick out a tempting destination from a colorful brochure, and mail off the deposit check! And Margaret and I could still savor the pleasure of reading about destinations on the itinerary with just as much anticipation and joy! Another consideration was that up until 1997 I was still acting in Chicago and every summer at the Peninsula Players, so it was very convenient to just fit in a tour or cruise sometime in the Spring or Fall; and, most importantly, a Caribbean cruise in the depths of the Chicago winter!

Anyone who knows me is aware that I enjoy food, and on cruise ships delectable meals are the rule. The usual scenario is on the first night you are seated around a dining room table with two or three other couples, everyone introduces themselves and says where they're from—Iowa or Minnesota or whatever—and then slightly after the salad course, the men open with that sure-fire conversational gambit of,

"Well, what do you do for a living?"

"Oh, I'm a dentist!" or

"I have a printing business!"

And then when it's my turn, I say,

"I'm an actor!"

A slightly embarrassed silence often follows this statement because most people have never met an actor, let alone talked with one. Men, especially, can be at a complete loss for what to say next. But eventually one of them clears his throat and takes up the gauntlet,

"Oh…that's interesting. Do you…hmm…do you get paid for doing that?"

And my usual answer is,

"Well, it's better than selling shoes!"

This usually gets a laugh or two, somewhat clears the air, and demonstrates that I'm just a regular guy with a sense of humor, even.

So this is my standard dialogue—my opening night lines—so to speak, on every new cruise; and Margaret, my long-suffering wife who has heard all my good lines delivered, ad nauseum, always manages to laugh at my jokes or at least smiles tolerantly. However, one night when I had delivered this standard line and the resulting laughter had died down, a gentleman sitting at our table said quietly,

"You know…*I sell shoes*!"

For the past twenty years we have traveled all over the world usually taking two or even three trips a year! Anytime

I saw a good bargain on a Caribbean cruise, off we'd go to the Virgin Islands, Bahamas, Antigua, Martinique, Jamaica, St. Lucia, Barbados, or Grenada! We've cruised through the Panama Canal twice; visited Cancun, Cozumel, Ixtapa, Guadalajara, Mazatlan and Acapulco, Mexico. Twice we've gone to South America: first a week's stay in Rio de Janeiro, and later on a cruise that went south from Valparaiso, Chile, around Cape Horn where the wind was so powerful I could barely stand up, then on to Tierra del Fuego, the Falkland Islands and finally Buenos Aires, Argentina. We had several cruises to Morocco and Spain visiting Costa del Sol, Costa Blanca, Costa Brava, Costa Calida and Barcelona. I'm very fond of Majorca, the Balearic island in the Mediterranean with its Moorish architecture, Crusader castles, and rocky coasts, and also the island of Malta, steeped in the history of both St. Paul and the Crusades.

In Fall of 1983 we had a memorable month-long Scandinavian visit: the highlight was 11 days along the Norway coast with the steamer, "Kong Olav" which sailed from Bergen to 300 miles north of the Artic circle, past the Lofoten Islands to the port of Kirkenes on the Barents Sea, with a side tour of Lapland.

In 1989 we toured through Eastern Europe: Yugoslavia, Romania, Hungary, Greece, Istanbul, Vienna. The following year we had an eighteen-day bus tour through Russia which followed the route which Hitler took during the German invasion in World War II: Berlin, Warsaw, Minsk, Smolensk, Moscow, Kalinin, St. Petersburg. When the trip finally ended in Helsinki, it was like breathing fresh air again! Afterwards we had planned an Alpine tour that included the Passion Play in Oberammergau—an amazing experience for us—but towards the tour's end tragedy struck. In Titisee, Black Forest, Margaret stumbled and broke her ankle, and we had to cut our trip short.

We toured Israel in 1992, and stayed in the Seven Arches Hotel owned by Palestinians on the Mount of Olives overlooking the golden domes of Jerusalem and the Garden of Gethsemane. We are grateful that we visited the Holy Land then because it would be impossible to do so now.

In 1985 and again in 1998 we cruised the Mediterranean visiting Athens, Corfu, Rhodes, Crete, Istanbul, Venice and Rome.

We went to Alaska in 1988, toured China in 1992, and later that year, New Zealand and Australia.

Our final overseas trips were in the millennium year of 2000 when in March we went on a seventeen-day Australian cruise to Brisbane, Cairns, Great Barrier Reef, Darwin, Bali, Java and Singapore. Two months later in May we sailed again to French Polynesia in the South Pacific.

My traveling days are probably numbered now; however, whenever a tempting travel brochure arrives in the mail I suddenly hear the familiar bells of the gypsy wagon that has a pair of alluring women who seem to beckon to me, crooning, "Come along with us and we'll carry you off to exotic lands across the oceans where you'll see strange and wonderful sights: ancient temples and fairytale castles, we'll fly over mountains, across deserts and through jungles to lost civilizations where fresh adventures await you!"

So I willingly succumb to their enticements, pick up the phone and start to dial for reservations. Lately, however, there is this equally insistent voice of Margaret's—the voice of common sense and reason—which says,

"Rob, how will we get through O'Hare and all those other airports?"

Or, another version is:

"Rob, people in their mid-eighties have no business driving across the country by themselves!"

So regretfully, I put away the travel brochures for now at least, but you never know when the gypsies might reappear.

Chapter 15
The Final Act

Ifeel very fortunate that at my age I can still vividly recall events that occurred over eighty years ago, and it has given me much pleasure to revisit those memories for the purpose of this autobiography. I don't have any serious regrets in my life. My goal was always to become the best actor I could be, given my abilities, not necessarily the most famous. I haven't done enough Shakespeare—only four or five plays—but otherwise as an actor, I'm grateful that I've had the opportunity to inhabit the mind and body of so many fascinating characters while onstage: doctors, lawyers, psychiatrists, judges, Irishmen (sober or otherwise), Nazis, murderers, villains, vampires, cuckolds, lounge lizards, sophisticates, kings, squires, knights, aristocratic dowagers, clowns, old men, very old men, and all manner of ecclesiastical hierarchy from priests, prelates, curates, bishops, cardinals, Popes and even God himself, and then descending to the Devil, and finally, Death!

As a young actor you are often dealing with rejection. You audition for a part, and it is given to someone else—that's the name of the game. However, once I became middle-aged, directors would usually seek me out because I had a solid reputation in Chicago as a good character actor with a strong work ethic. In my theatrical career, I never needed an agent. I have always cultivated a philosophy of optimism, and have tried to maintain a sense of humor. Without these you'd commit suicide! My attitude towards auditions was that if I didn't get the part, it meant I'd be available when something else turned up which might be even better!

Naturally, I might have liked to have had more Broadway exposure, but there are always trade-offs in life, and working in Chicago has enabled me to lead a sane and rewarding family life. I have been fortunate in my marriage to Margaret who has been my friend and confidante for 57 years. We have been supportive of each other's careers: hers as a musician and mine in the theatre. We are also pleased that our three children have turned out well. David has been a scientist at NASA for the past twenty years: he and his wife, Haze, live in California and are manic mountain climbers, cyclists, skiers and own several horses. Our daughter, Kay Friedrich, lives in Pensacola, Florida where she teaches ballet, plays the flute, is the mother of two grown daughters, Shelley and Carrie, and is married to Doug, a psychology professor. Our youngest, Don, is a gifted stained-glass artist and owner of the Door County Bakery along with his multi-talented wife, Jean. He also plays the guitar, sings, dances and performed at the Players in *Pump Boys and Dinettes* in 1995.

When we moved to Door County with its many concerts and cultural opportunities, it was the beginning of another grand adventure in our lives. We have thoroughly enjoyed it and are probably more active now than we would have been in Chicago because we don't have to deal with hectic expressway traffic; and Margaret is much in demand here as a violinist in church recitals, musical productions at Door Auditorium, and other venues. We actively volunteer for various community groups: Door Auditorium, Peninsula Music Festival, and others as a way of becoming involved in our new community and making new friends. But beyond all that activity, we are exhilarated with just the joy of living on this beautiful peninsula: the dramatic October skies, trees brilliant with russets and gold, wild waves racing across Green Bay, or the quiet winters when the ice- bound harbor glistens with sunlight—it is an ever-changing panorama of beauty! Just the gentle contentment of observing wildlife in our own backyard—birds at the feeder, deer amongst the hostas, or even marauding raccoons—brings us pleasure. I like to garden and even though I can't do it myself anymore, there are landscapers who have transformed our garden into an oasis of serenity.

We are blessed with many Door County friends, and we attend and support several churches. Although I probably can't travel the high seas anymore, we enjoy doing bus tours like a trip to Mackinac Island, or the Tulip Festival in Holland, Michigan, or a cultural tour to Milwaukee's Art Museum. Life is continually interesting, especially when you involve yourself with other people.

This summer I will be acting at the Players in the role of Cardinal Wolsey in *A Man for All Seasons* about Henry VIII's divorce petition to the Church of England. At my venerable age they have elevated me to a cardinal and I told the directors, Todd Schmidt and Greg Vinkler, that in keeping with my exalted position, my costume must include a very impressive bishop's mitre! As long as I can still totter around the stage, I'll be happy acting up until the very end. And when I look into the mirror, I still have all my hair, my bountiful silvery locks … time has not altered that, at least!

Our revels now are ended. These actors,
As I foretold you, were all spirits and are
Melted into air, into thin air.
And, like the baseless fabric of this vision,
The cloud-capped towers, the gorgeous palaces,
The solemn temples, the great globe itself—
Yeah, all which inherit—shall dissolve
And, like this insubstantial pageant faded,
Leave not a rack behind. We are such stuff
As dreams are made on, and our little life
Is rounded with a sleep.

—William Shakespeare, *The Tempest*

No two shows are alike in the making. Each show is a living piece of your life in a small unreal world with its own character, integrity, and its own new set of memorable happenings. You begin to love and adapt to its strangeness. Dreams harden into substance. Values seem to come into focus. You wish it would never end but the show does end. The dream world vanishes with it, and back you land in the real world with a thud—drained, uneasy, jittery, and difficult to get along with. There is only one cure—a new show! A small, new, unreal world with new visions, experiences, and incredible happenings. Again you love it, adapt to it, and wish it would never end, but end it does. Another part of you vanishes… that is Show Business!

— Author Unknown

"Esse Quam Videre" ("To be, rather than to seem")
—The Thompson Family Motto

Chapter 16
Interviews

Todd Schmidt: Executive Producer, Peninsula Players

Greg Vinkler: Artistic Director and Actor

Tom Mula: Playwright and Actor

Amy McKenzie: Actress, Director

Maggy Magerstadt Rosner: Retired Actress

James Maronek: Scenic Designer

Richard Christiansen: Retired Theatre Critic,
  Chicago Tribune

Eleanor Moyer: Bob's Sister

Margaret Thompson: Wife

David Thompson: Son

Kay Friedrich: Daughter

Don Thompson: Son

Todd Schmidt: *Executive Producer, Peninsula Players*

Bob Thompson has this great ability to connect with the audience…he just radiates a fun, warm, mischievous quality that's brilliant! His ability to work and know how to make the audience respond is masterful! For example, in *A Funny Thing Happened on the Way to the Forum* his character was supposed to be walking around the Seven Hills of Rome so Bob, dressed in a Roman toga, is circling around the audience and every time he'd walk in front of the stage he'd intone in this quavery voice "second time around!" (Bob gave the word "around" about seven syllables). The audience just went crazy!!

He had the lead role as Martin Vanderhof in *You Can't Take it With You* in 1995, and it was one of our top selling shows. In *Guys and Dolls* he sang a rather sweet, sentimental song and he was somewhat nervous about doing the role because he's not a musical-comedy actor, but he stole the show! It was a lovely moment and the audience just melted.

In *Witness for the Prosecution* he plays a doddery old magistrate with a wig who suddenly perks up and says, "this was a strawberry blonde?" Again, the words "strawberry blonde" were wonderfully elongated; his ability to use language is phenomenal! He's very good in Ray Cooney farces because his comic timing is impeccable. There are actors here like Greg Vinkler and Tom Mula who have studied Bob while they're working with him. There's a kind of seasoning or true apprenticeship of having an older character actor who is passing on his skills just by other actors observing him.

The Peninsula Players has a unique magic about the place. Theatre itself is a collaborative art form with actors, directors, designers, technicians and box office all working together. Everyone is here because they love what they do…it is a feeling of people working for the common good. Then the setting of doing five shows within a certain time frame on a limited budget where everyone is working together, living together, eating together—it becomes the ultimate way to produce theatre because you're inundated with it, you're living and breathing it and everyone is working towards the same goal. To get a group of people focused on the same ideal, it produces the incredible results which happen at the Players. Add to that the beautiful setting on the Green Bay shores with its westerly sunset views, being in a remote, self contained setting, even within Door County, where maybe a week goes by and you don't even leave the property. You get up in the morning, you have your meals, you walk down to the shore, you do your work, you do the show at night, you hang out around the fire after the show, then you go to bed. You could easily go a week here and not have left the property.

Then you bring in audiences who have been coming here for years or their parents came here, they've summered in Door County, and the Players is part of their family tradition. It just adds up to be the perfect ingredients for doing theatre. The audiences here are always ready to have a good time: they're on vacation, they're more relaxed, they're not worried about getting mugged in the parking lot, or that their car might be stolen, or that they have struggled with cabs or restaurants as you might in a big city, and they haven't paid $75 to see a show. If it's a nice night with a sunset or a fire in the firepit, and the bar is open—it creates a feeling of magic and everyone is caught up in the spirit of the theatre and this has gone on for 68 seasons!!

Greg Vinkler: *Artistic Director*

I've learned a lot from Bob Thompson particularly in comedy. Bob does a lot with body language and sounds, which is a kind of expressiveness, a kind of working outside of the script.

One of my favorite memories of Bob was we were doing Alan Ayckbourne's *Tons of Money* and Bob was playing a gardener. His first entrance was when he came through the French windows with a basket of eggs, put them on a chair, and then walked out again. All he had was one word, "Eggs". On opening night Amy McKenzie and I are doing the scene, we hear a knock on the door, Bob comes through the door, gets entrance applause, he puts the basket of eggs down on the table and says, "Eggggs!" with about *17 syllables*. The audience goes crazy with more applause, then he walks out and on his exit, gets applause again. That's three rounds of applause for one word—he's a master of comedy!

Bob has an amazing memory not only for lines—he is always word perfect in his lines. You can always be comfortable with him on stage, he's always there, he always makes his entrances, he's completely reliable as an actor, and considering how old he is, it's remarkable!

One of the wonderful things about the Players is because we all eat, sleep, work together in the same campus, there's a mixture of old and young men and women, really experienced actors and beginners who come together. Todd and I try to make everyone feel that they're important, that they all have something to offer, and that just because you're an intern doesn't make you low man on the totem pole. We encourage people to mix so that the younger can gain knowledge from the more experienced members like Bob. We have these young kids who have this exuberance, energy and desire for knowledge which is very refreshing—it's a good balance. There are no "stars" walking around, we want everyone to mix and be treated equally well. Everyone is important, everyone has a contribution to make. We tell the interns that we can't do this without them, that their backstage work of painting scenery or doing props is essential to the success of the production.

We are aware that there are some tourists who come up and only want to see comedies or musicals. There are a lot of shows we have done where the audience had a great time laughing through the show but the minute they walked out the door, they couldn't tell you what it was about. One of my favorite things is to look into the audience and see them laugh. That to me is the gift that we can give people. But it's also wonderful to do shows where people walk out of the theatre and think about something they haven't thought about before. So it's important that we don't give them just "cotton candy" all the time!

Tom Mula: *Actor and Playwright*

My impetus in writing the play *Bob Almighty* was to show off Bob's abilities, which are considerable. I put the main character in a wheelchair so it wouldn't be so physically taxing for an older man. The play was funny and heart warming and played to all of Bob's strengths. It was unfortunate timing: he had just gone through a life-threatening operation and moved from his Downers Grove home to Door County—two of the most traumatic events a person could experience. Bob looked at all the lines in the script including a list—actors hate lists because they're difficult to memorize. I told him that the list could be written on a piece of paper which he could keep in his pocket. However, Bob was concerned that he wouldn't be able to get his lines under his belt in time, and so after some very difficult soul searching, he decided to pass on it. I know this was a very painful decision for him.

The play was written for Bob with his voice and his strengths in mind and also for an audience who has known him for 20 or 30 years. I think Howard Witt did an excellent job; but if Bob had done it, it would have been a transcendent experience!

Bob is pretty amazing onstage. The first few times you work with him, it's a revelation! You are looking at sixty years of craft, which is an awesome thing. I know that all of us steal from him because he's developed a "shtick" over the years, which is priceless and needs to be preserved. I know that Greg Vinkler has gotten great mileage out of his "Bob Thompsonisms" and so have I. In fact, in my one-man show, "Jacob Marley's Christmas Carol", I use Bob for one of my characters and it always irritates me that that character gets a better audience reaction than the other ones!

Bob is really a master comedian. I remember him in the Ray Cooney play, *It Runs in the Family*, where Bob is an old man in a wheelchair and he imagines that this young nurse is actually his bride who left him years ago but who has returned. He was imagining that he was on a second honeymoon, and every eye in the audience was watching him and they were just howling! It was priceless shtick!

It is a wonderful thing to be exposed to that level of craft. Us younger scavengers are stealing the good stuff and with Bob there certainly is a lot to steal. People used to talk about how Laurence Olivier's "Hamlet" was influenced by John Barrymore's portrayal, and Kenneth Branaugh borrowed from Olivier. This is an acting tradition, and younger actors will always go to these resources.

I think that actors, in general, get by on sort of a blessed egotism. That's how actors survive because you need a pretty resilient ego just to handle all the rejection an actor gets from so many sources. So being willing to put yourself out there, whether it be an audition or performing on stage, takes a pretty healthy ego.

The Mystery of Irma Vep was my first show at the Players in the fall of 1993. This was before the new actors' housing had been built and they had this scary, ramshackle looking place down by the water and I thought to myself, "Oh my God, I've committed myself to working in 'Dogpatch' for the next eight weeks!" However, I instantly fell in love with the place. The Players is just a blessing for actors. Jim McKenzie wanted to make it a good place for actors to work, and the theatre gets the cream of the crop of talent from the Midwest and both coasts. Greg and Todd are always careful to hire "happy campers" because you're in such a pressure cooker to crank out these plays so quickly that it's really important that everyone get along with each other. One bad apple can really spoil the whole experience for everybody. So it's a very social situation where you're working, living, and eating together and you don't have many private moments during the day. You have this situation where you're doing terrific work, you're in this astonishingly beautiful setting and that's so important. It's a very special place in the quiet cedar forest, and when you go to bed at night you can hear the waves on the shore.

Amy McKenzie: *Actress, Director, Daughter of Jeanne Bolan and Jim McKenzie*

I was born at the tail end of vaudeville only in the sense that there was still "bus and truck", still one night stands—little theatre companies getting sent out from New York, traveling across the country, going to where the work was. In those days, of course, my family moved no less than three times a year; we had stage trunks and they got tied to the roof of our station wagon and off we went! Anyone who has tasted the "wine" of theatre, even peripherally I believe, is changed and has a different relationship to the outside world forever after. The theatre world is almost its own tribe and removed from civilian life rather like a gypsy encampment—I was raised like a gypsy. I went to no less than three schools a year so for me the Players was home—it was the one constant, the place we always returned to, and it was the epitome of the best theatre I ever witnessed, be it New York, California, Connecticut or Florida.

In the early 1960's when my parents took over the theatre, because of small audiences there were always desperate times. We promoted the shows with handbills and we had a policy in those days that if you had at least as many people in the audience as there were onstage, we did the show! We only began to see consistently full houses in the 1990's. Prior to that, it was always dicey. We were constantly aware of the fact that if something went wrong, we had no pre-season nest egg, there was nothing to ensure the future of the theatre. It was very scary. I cleaned bathrooms for years, did concessions, passed out handbills. I started ushering when I was four, and did bathrooms when I was seven. We were there and you had to work, there was no choice, everyone had to work. Of course, nowadays, because of increased tourist traffic, ticket sales cover 90% of the theatre budget, which is virtually unheard of in any arts organization.

My brother, Kevin McKenzie, is a technical master extraordinaire, electrician and lighting director. During the tornado of 1998, he did an incredible service for the Players; in fact, the show would not have gone on if Kevin hadn't been there. When the lights went out during the height of the storm, he got into his RV and drove it to the upper parking lot, and then he climbed up onto the theatre roof. Let me tell you, when I ventured outside it felt like someone was pouring buckets of water on my head! He climbed up onto that slippery roof and performed some emergency electrical triage with cables from his RV generator to provide power to the theatre so the performance could continue. It was *extremely dangerous*, you don't fiddle with electricity in the rain, let alone in a bloody tornado! It was unbelievably heroic!! Later, we laughed about it and said, "There you are risking your life again for the theatre!" We were all raised in the theatre *and the show must go on*!!

One of Bob Thompson's greatest virtues as a director was he let an actor act. He didn't spend a lot of time discussing the motivation or indulging in the inner work necessary which sometimes can be so much sophistry. Not to say that it isn't important but, particularly in summer stock, it could be inappropriate. He knew what the goal was, he knew how to get a play up in one week of rehearsal time. It's tremendous pressure because you're directing almost every play during the season. He knew how to articulate what he wanted because he was a first-rate actor himself. He also knew the folly of giving acting lessons to anyone during that period and he never allowed himself the indulgence of showing off to the rest of the company, which he might have done because he was certainly capable of it. The man could take stage in one word! The greatest example of that was in the farce *Tons of Money* where he had one word, "eggs". Bob could command the audience with just one word, that says it all!

Of course, that was in his comic range, but he has an equally developed dramatic side, which is compelling. I'll never forget his performance in *Da*—he embodied that role and it was an honor to be in that show with him. It was irresistible to watch him and there were several times I was in the wings holding back tears. It was just beautiful! In *Painting Churches* with Bob and Jean Sincere, it was a really special experience for me to play their daughter on stage and they were both certainly theatrical parents to me in many ways. Over the years I learned so much from watching them, their relationship came through so beautifully. Another example of that was *On Golden Pond* in which, I believe, Bob Thompson and Jean Sincere were the epitome of both characters! Bob Thompson has given us such a rich library of memories and in such a tremendous range of roles—he is a thinking man's actor!

As a director, Bob would allow you to have your time to be in the discovering process without breathing down your neck. Of course, you want a director's attention and their input. I remember a speech or two that I wasn't getting and then he sat down and picked it apart with me, and helped me build it like a piece of music. When I needed help, there was no question that I got his fullest attention but when I was getting it on my own, he left me alone and that's invaluable. Nowadays, directors are seen as more and more important. Sometimes when a director's vision supercedes that of the play, I believe that to be inappropriate. That was never a problem with Bob; he wasn't ego-driven. As an actress I really began to appreciate that in later years when I had experiences with other directors throughout the country whom I would describe as meddling. If you get in an actor's way too soon in their process, telling them what you want the outcome to be and not trusting that they will find their way there, you can interfere to the point that the actors never organically discover the character for themselves so they never believe in it. It could be disastrous! There is that deep intuitiveness about acting that's very fragile. The actor might never find their path again, and as director you might get what you want, but it's not ever going to have the same resonance for the audience as if it had been fully developed organically by that actor. It might look right but it won't feel the same.

My mother died in 1976 shortly before Bob came to direct that summer and it was a very fragile time for me. He was very supportive. He has been quite a mentor to me and I have the greatest respect for him and the deepest love.

Jean Sincere is an incredibly special woman and over the years has given me advice that was monumentally important for me in understanding the world and what was happening around me. She was blunt and never pulled any punches. She is a very strong woman, eternally kind, and lives up to her name.

Jean and I were doing a play together, we were onstage and I had said my line and then she didn't respond. I turned to look at her and she was as white as a ghost, her mouth was hanging open, and she was speechless. My first thought was "Oh my God, she's had a stroke!" I was deathly afraid of what was happening so I ushered her offstage to the stage manager, and then came back on and began ad-libbing the entire scene, somehow making the connection to the scene that would follow. When I finally got offstage I said,

"Jean, what happened, are you all right?"

She said, "I'm fine…it wasn't…Oh God, Amy!"

"What is it?"

"I looked over at you and when you did that move… you…I saw Jeanne… it wasn't even you anymore. It wasn't as if you reminded me of her…it was Jeanne—I saw Jeanne!"

And later she began to doubt what she saw, "Maybe it was just so much like something she would have done…"

But I guess I just reminded her so much of my mother in that moment that it shocked her senseless. That was an unforgettable moment!

Caroline Rathbone was the most magnetic person I have ever met, she could charm a blade of grass, she was incredible—everyone was in love with her. Our families were close and my father would do anything for her. During her final year when she was bedridden I did one day a week taking care of her. She used to have me model some of her clothes and she actually gave me some incredible outfits because they fit me. She taught me how to do the model walk, she'd say, "Amy, you have to walk this way, darling."

Even though she was bedridden and virtually incapacitated, she was still delightful, entertaining, and funny to visit. Both she and Maggy Magerstadt Rosner are my idea of grande dames who could do anything they chose to do. Talk about role models! For me it has been so interesting to have grown up in the theatre with the contrast of being at poverty's edge with catastrophe lurking just around the corner and then, at the same time, experiencing "champagne and caviar"!

Maggy Magerstadt Rosner: *Peninsula Players Actress 1940-71*

I first came to the Players in 1940 as a 17-year-old apprentice. Prior to that I had been kind of a "kiddie actor" in Chicago. I think I must have been a rather poisonous child, very obstreperous and a cunning mimic. When I was 9 or 10, people were always telling me, "Oh, you should be an actor!" I liked to imitate some of my mother's friends and it could be quite embarrassing for her, if not downright annoying.

I remember we had a wonderful black cook who had delicious malapropisms. One day she and my mother were planning a dinner party and there were cookbooks spread all over the kitchen table. The menu was already set but they were having trouble choosing the dessert. Finally Ruby said,

"Miz M...you know how Mr. Magerstadt do loves his 'Baked Elastics'!"

Or occasionally when they'd run out of some ingredient, Ruby would say,

"Don't you worry, Miz M, I'll just put on my turbine and run over to the A&P and pick it up!"

I was fascinated with language. Finally, my mother took me to our pediatrician who suggested that,

"Why don't we channel some of these tendencies and have her take elocution lessons!"

So you can see it was practically a prescription! My mother brought me to the doyenne of Chicago's elocution teachers, a Miss Luella Bartham, who affected a high pitched, slightly hysterical British accent, and after two or three years of diligent study, my language skills were properly refined.

In 1940 when I applied to be an apprentice, Caroline Rathbone came to visit me with Gertrude Needham, an English actress who must have strayed into the Midwest, ran out of work and got stranded here. She was one of the original actresses at the Players and, in addition to performing, she acted as a chaperone to the young apprentices and taught them voice and diction skills.

I loved performing at the Players, I loved the camaraderie but was ambivalent about my career. I went to New York as a young actress and I had a lot of connections but disliked the auditions and "cattle calls". There were so many other areas besides theatre that interested me such as travel. I frequently went to Europe from January through May and visited Italy, Spain, and Germany, which in those days was quite cheap.

During the 1969 Christmas season, I visited Rodion and Caroline Rathbone in Saudi Arabia as part of a much-anticipated trip to East Africa. To visit Saudi Arabia it was necessary for me to apply for a visa and I was crushed when the Saudi embassy refused me saying they preferred not to have "a solitary foreign woman" entering their kingdom so, instead, I met Caroline and Rodion for a three-day visit in that magical city, Beirut. However, Rodion still fretted over my visa, so we approached the Saudi embassy in Beirut where we played the family angle. I was, after all, Rodion and Caroline's sister-in-law because in 1956 I had been married briefly to Richard Fisher—and there was the religious aspect of the upcoming Christian holiday, so in the end the embassy relented.

Two days later, I was on a plane to Saudi Arabia and, per Rodion's suggestion, when I went through Customs, a copy of *Playboy* magazine was prominently displayed inside my suitcase which the smiling Customs officials immediately confiscated, actually arguing over who could peruse it first, and then they allowed me into their country.

The weather in Jiddah was fiercely hot, nevertheless Rodion counseled me to wear long sleeves, long skirt and a headscarf in order to be decently covered so as not to offend any Saudi sensibilities. Few women were evident on the streets except at the bazaar, which was packed with fruit and vegetable stalls, gold merchants, and all manner of exotic merchandise. The city was a peculiar combination of the ancient and the ultra moderne. Near the bazaar, a camel circled endlessly hooked to a primitive water wheel, men on stringed cots lounged in the shade while women pounded grain on stone mortars, or were sequestered on rooftops away from undesirable male glances.

An elaborate holiday feast was being prepared by Dounia Rathbone, their daughter, who had flown in from London, and the dinner concluded with typical English Christmas "crackers" and a plum pudding from Harrods! Potent cocktails of "seddiki juice", the Saudi vernacular for bootlegged spirits, made the evening especially merry!!

Bob Thompson directed in the 1953-57 seasons when I was performing. While at the Goodman, he had received wonderful training and knew a lot of stage craft, how to block a play, how to move the actors around. His demeanor was always calm and he treated people civilly. However, he had what I would call "a little porcine imp" within him and occasionally when on stage he'd let that demon jump out, and when he did, it was 'pure proscuitto'! He is much beloved by his audiences and has given them almost sixty-five years of wonderful characters!

James Maronek: *Scenic Designer, Professor Emeritus, DePaul University*

In 1950 I was a student at the Goodman Theatre School when someone from the theatre called and said they need-ed a set designer at the Players that summer. I took the train to Two Rivers, and then the bus dropped me off at the Players billboard on Highway 42 in Fish Creek. I walked down to the theatre where I was met by Mama Fisher who took one look at me and said,

"You're the set designer? *You're too young*!

And she was right, I *was* too young: I was only 17.

However, for me, the theatre was love at first sight. I fell in love with the Players, I couldn't get enough of the place, and I returned for four seasons until 1953!

I became very close to the Fisher family. Richie was, of course, a genius and a profound influence on me, artistically, because he possessed impeccable taste. He was supremely intelligent, theatrically talented, and as resident set design-er he and I worked together constantly. He helped me develop as an artist and, for me, it was a marvelous experi-ence. He was imperious, he was great and he knew it! Artistically, he ran the theatre like a tight ship and everyone did their best, and then some.

Caroline was a genius in her own way; I think she invent-ed the concept of networking because she had friends all over the county. She knew everybody and could ask favors from anyone. In those days, the glue which held everything together was handbills: the shows were advertised on cheap paper flyers. Caroline would stop at every place of business from Sturgeon Bay to Gills Rock—she had hundreds of these flyers in the back of her car and I was one of the primary distributors. I got to know every nook and cranny of the peninsula as I accompanied her on this route. Along the way she'd stop and talk to people, listen to their problems, which paid off in spades because when she needed a prop for a show, she'd remember that she'd seen something in somebody's living room, and she'd ask if she could borrow it. And, of course, they were thrilled to see their stuff onstage. She'd give out complimentary tickets to anybody and everybody along the way. Everybody knew her and loved her. Her acting was more bluster than talent but it didn't matter because she'd just bulldoze her way through a role and everybody loved it!

Mama Fisher was of strong German stock; there was a resident cook but Mama supervised the kitchen, which was dominated by a huge wood-fired stove. She was the "mother" of everyone in the company.

Papa Fisher was eccentric, he was the company handyman, constantly puttering and fixing to keep the machinery running. He had a garage that was lined with shelves that were stacked with cigar boxes—all of them unlabeled. They were filled with screws, nails, nuts and bolts, washers; and if I needed something, I'd walk over and he knew *immediately* where something was located. One of his quirks was he was addicted to drinking vinegar and kept a bottle hidden in the garage. When he drank it, his bald head would begin to sweat, and when Mama noticed this she'd exclaim,

"You've been drinking vinegar again, haven't you!"

One of my treasured memories was on moonlit nights, Armand, the Rathbone's dog, and I used to go out at midnight and dance with the bats. They would swoop through the air just above our heads and Armand would leap for joy, trying to catch them. It was an utterly mystical experience.

One of my duties at the Players, besides set design and handbill distribution, was I was required to perform as an extra onstage in large cast productions. My last show was *Born Yesterday* when I laid down the law and told Caroline I would never set foot on stage in front of an audience again because performing was not my thing!

Another of my duties was on rainy nights I stood at the back of the theatre with a long pole and walked up and down the rows, poking at the canvas roof so no rain would seep through onto the audience's heads.

In 1952, I came to visit the Rathbones when they were living in a cabin on the property that winter. As a special treat, Caroline cooked me an elaborate gourmet dinner with all my favorite foods on her woodstove. Rodion had flown in from Saudi Arabia and the two of us along with their dog hiked out to Hat Island across the ice and snow.

During my fourth season at the theatre I received a notice from my draft board—it was in the middle of the season and the timing couldn't have been worse. Besides that, I was a conscientious objector so I had a problem. I needed to go to Milwaukee, my hometown, to convince the draft board that I should get a CO classification and in those days that was not an easy thing to do. It was also a risky thing to do, too, and the penalties were severe if you failed.

Bob Thompson and Caroline were like surrogate parents to me, they counseled me about this matter and ultimately, the three of us drove down to Milwaukee so I could keep my appointment with the draft board. Then we drove back again in the same day which, before the days of interstate highways, was no mean feat. It was an arduous trip through every small town along the route: Grafton, Saukville, Sheboygan, Two Rivers, etc. I was so grateful that they took me under their wing during that anxious time. I was granted a CO status and served as a medic in Korea.

In later years my wife was on the Joseph Jefferson awards committee and we were obliged to see six shows a week, every week during the Chicago theatre season, so we had the opportunity to see both Bob Thompson and Bill Munchow many times. Bob's acting is unique. He has created a persona for himself that is so special and he is revered by everyone who has seen him. I think the best tribute is his son, Don's, imitation of him.

Richard Christiansen: *Retired Theatre Critic*, Chicago Tribune

Bob Thompson is an actor you can always enjoy because his pleasure in performing is so evident. Over the years I have seen him in many, many shows and his vigor, zest and gusto was always a delight. As an actor he was very important to Chicago theatre because he bridged generations. He worked at a time when there was very little resident theatre; and over time, as this grew, Bob Thompson grew with it. As one of Chicago's leading character actors, he has just blossomed.

Bob received the very first Joseph Jefferson award for Best Supporting Actor in 1968 for his performance as Linus Larrabee in *Sabrina Fair* starring Kathy Crosby at the Mill Run Theatre. More recently in 1994 he was seen as Martin Vanderhof in *You Can't Take it With You* at the Candlelight Forum Theatre, a role which seemed to be made for him. His obvious relish and joy in performing that character is a memory I shall always cherish.

Eleanor Moyer, *Bob's Sister*

My father was somewhat stern, led a very orderly existence, and GE was the most important thing in his life. The 1930's was the heyday of hydro-electric power development in this country; he had worked on the diesel generators at Boulder Dam on the Colorado River, and was present at the grand opening. My father had a fine bass baritone voice, spoke with excellent diction, and acted in church plays. I think he had hoped Bob might become an attorney. Garfield Park in the 1920's was a lovely neighborhood and I remember, when mother took us to the conservatory, the warm fragrance of the tropical flowers and the exotic palm trees.

My Aunt Faye had lost her job during the Depression so, for a period, she sold Rogiér cosmetics door to door. When she set out for work, she was carefully made up, dressed to the nines with her red hair tucked under a fetching hat. She had a personality that could light up any room she entered, and she was like a second mother to us. She had some nice boyfriends who took her to the Palmer House and fancy restaurants.

A favorite story of hers occurred in later years when she worked as a government stenographer in Springfield, Illinois. She had just boarded the train for Chicago and as she flounced down the aisle in one of her suits and an elegant, wide-brimmed hat, a young girl asked her,

"Are you a Senator's wife?"

She looked the part.

In May 1941, my brother, Rob, came to visit me for one weekend at Carleton College and during that time I was especially popular with my girlfriends when I introduced them to this handsome, single, 25-year-old New York actor.

I am my brother's greatest fan and supporter because as I watch him onstage—whether in comedy or serious drama— his spoken words, facial expressions and even his hands all portray his character in the play. Some of my favorite shows were: *Over the River and Through the Woods*, *Angel Street*, *Our Town*, *Status Quo Vadis*, *Da*, *God's Favorite*, *South Pacific*, and several British comedies. He always took center stage, no matter how small the part. He just commanded the stage and it was always a joy for me to watch him.

Margaret Thompson, *Bob's Wife*

When I was a music teacher in the 1940's in Downers Grove, I met Bob's sister, Eleanor, who was working at the same school and we became close friends. It was only after a year that she told me that she had a brother in the Air Force in Guam, so she mailed him a photograph of me standing next to his canoe without much explanation—I just happened to be in the photo and she didn't even say who I was. She arranged that we should begin writing each other and we did so for a year. By the time we met we knew pretty much everything about each other except whether we would actually like each other and that only took a few days. When he returned from the South Pacific on January 3, 1946, I was waiting for him on the train platform along with his family, and we were married the following June.

Downers Grove had an exceptionally strong music program and one of my extra duties as a new teacher was to teach tonettes (an instrument rather like a recorder) so the children would learn something about counting time and reading notes—then if they went on to a band or string instrument it wouldn't be so foreign to them. There was a boy in my 5th grade class named Sherrill Milnes and I soon realized he was pretty sharp musically. One of the tunes they had to learn was "Going Home" by Dvořák. After this lesson was over, he raised his hand and said,

"Miss Porter, that isn't really the right name for that tune...I know because we play that at home. It's called Dvořák's *New World Symphony!*"

His mother, Thelma Milnes, became my first adult friend through the school. She was a fine choral director and wonderful person who helped me organize a parents' association for the school orchestra. I taught beginning string instruments (starting in 5ᵗʰ grade) and within a year I had an orchestra going. I traveled to four different grade schools. Sherrill continued to take private violin lessons with me through high school. When my children were young I no longer taught school, but I had 15 or 20 private violin students, and taught three or four days a week in my home. I had another girl who was also quite good and she and Sherrill played the Bach *Double Concerto for Violin* in a state music competition and got first place! Sherrill was always very personable and grateful for help. He's retired from the Met now but still returns occasionally to Downers Grove even though he no longer has relatives living there. He teaches at Northwestern.

One of the ways that Bob and I are fairly well matched is that we were both performers. I, not to the professional level that he was, but I was the concertmistress of the Western Suburban Symphony in LaGrange for forty years and I did a lot of performing in church groups, oratorios, etc. I was a semi-professional musician but because we had different fields we never competed with each other and we both enjoyed seeing the other perform. We were both good listeners.

The only time I felt badly about Bob being in the theatre was when the kids had their various graduations and he was never able to attend any of them because he always had a show. He just couldn't say, "I'm not coming tonight because my son or daughter has graduation", nor could he turn down a good job of five or six weeks of work just because there's one night he couldn't be there.

Bob was a scoutmaster for the Cub Scouts and he was pretty active with the Boy Scouts so the boys had their dad around when they were involved in scouting. But when he was teaching at Rosary, they did three plays a year and much of the time he was staying for late rehearsals until ten o-clock at night and was not getting up at 7 am to see the kids off to school, so sometimes they didn't see their dad for most of the week. When the kids were in high school they used to watch him perform at Melody Top—we usually went to opening and closing nights. Of course, we saw many plays at the Peninsula Players and something like *On Golden Pond* which I loved, you could see it all your life!

In November 1975 when Bob was doing *Angel Street* in Chicago, he thought it would be nice to invite all of the cast (they were all from out of town) to our Downers Grove home for Thanksgiving dinner. There were 23 of them plus our own family so I roasted two turkeys and in addition to our dining room table, which seated 12, and a large table in the family room, we also set up two card tables in front of the living room fireplace. There had been a terrible snowstorm the night before so Bob, along with our son-in-law, had arranged to pick up the cast from the North side of Chicago. Kay's daughter, Shelley, was in a highchair then and I remember she was shooting peas all over the floor, but somehow we all managed to have a good time. I didn't have a dishwasher in that home so afterwards, everyone lined up to help wash dishes in the kitchen and Dina Merrill was right out there helping to dry.

But driving home afterwards they all got stuck in the snow in the unplowed side streets. It was quite a memorable experience!

David Thompson, *Bob's Son*

I think my father had a very strong view of parenting based on what he felt was his own father's lack of involvement. On weekends, he'd take us ice-skating at Morton Arboretum, which was a sport he enjoyed. He was a good skater and a real athlete. As young children, he also took us skiing; he had an old pair of wooden skis. When my brother, Don, and I were in Junior and Senior High we did ski racing and every weekend my parents drove us to ski hills near Baraboo, Wisconsin, or Boyne, Michigan. When my father was in a play, my mother would drive us to Petoskey, Michigan, near Boyne, which was a 400 mile, eight hour drive. We'd leave Downers Grove after school on Friday and arrive about midnight. I remember many winters of horrible snowstorms where there'd be a foot of snow on the highway. We'd ski all day Saturday and Sunday afternoon until 4 pm and then drive home again. As kids we thought this was normal; we didn't realize until years later how unusual this was, nor the degree of time, energy and commitment it required of our parents.

Similarly, we went tent camping almost every summer. In 1962 we did a five or six week tour of the Pacific Northwest, visiting Lake Louise and Banff and returning through the Southwest. Generally when we'd reach a campsite, we three kids disappeared into the woods, leaving all the set-up work to my parents. By the time I entered college, we had traveled to almost every state besides Canada.

I have strong memories of my father's Aunt Faye, a huge flamboyant Dutch woman just covered in lipstick! I knew she had worked for Admiral Byrd and later had some government job in Springfield, Illinois. However, in our minds she might as well have been the secretary to President Lincoln—she was larger than life and also a big traveler like my dad. Some weekends she took the train up from Springfield, we'd meet her on the platform, and she'd smother us with kisses, which we usually tried to avoid.

When I was a student at UCLA I used to bicycle fifty miles to Oxnard to visit my father's cousin, Margit Hegedus Cave. She always told me that she and her sister had studied with Zoltan Kodaly at the Budapest Conservatory and that the impresario, Sol Hurok, had brought them to America. In the 1930's she and her husband, Don Cave, had moved to Hollywood where she was a violinist with the CBS Symphony doing musical scores for the film industry.

As children, all three of us grew up in the theatre. We did

a lot of walk-on stuff at Rosary College. When I was in high school, I played the part of the narrator in *Our Town*, and also danced in some musical comedy numbers at Rosary. I had seen John Kriza, the premier dancer from American Ballet Theatre perform at the Melody Top Theatre. We all viewed theatre as just another club like being in the band or orchestra. It was an interesting way to grow up because other people viewed acting as something which required special talent with tremendous accolades but, for us, it was just normal or commonplace.

Dad never wanted any of us to go into the arts. He would always say, "Don't count on anything…it's a bad life, it's difficult, and you won't make any money!" So all three of us were always very talented in the arts but Dad didn't want us to go into it!

Kay Friedrich, *Bob's Daughter*

In the 1950's we were just young children when we stayed at the Peninsula Players, and I have vivid memories of the mice in our cabins. We always wanted to make pets of them and I couldn't understand why my mother wanted to get rid of them—why finding a mouse made her freak out. When she put us to bed at night, she used to say "If you'll be real quiet, you can hear Daddy talking onstage," which, of course, was true because the cabins were just a stone's throw from the theatre. One of the best things was that the morning after a performance, we kids used to make a bee-line for the theatre to look for coins beneath the seats. There'd be all kinds of money that had fallen out of men's pockets! Everyone in the dorms and cabins used the community bathroom, which was an absolutely spooky place. You entered directly from the woods, it was dark and there could be anything lurking in there—spiders, skunks, boogey-men!

My dad was a family man and working at Rosary College

allowed him to support and raise his children. My father was always very unpretentious, you'd never guess that he was an actor. He was very involved with the Downers Grove community, very active in the Methodist Church. We usually only saw him on weekends because he came home late after a rehearsal or a show, and mornings he'd be still asleep when we left for school. Rosary College was fun for us. Every year they'd put on these fabulous Christmas parties. The nuns were fun and, in particular, Sister Gregory—she was just a hoot! My dad always played the piano at cast parties, and Sister Gregory would hold a martini glass filled with water and an olive and pretend she was smashed!

My dad loved planning our camping trips, he'd get out all the maps and study them. He has an absolute "wanderlust" and even last week he was talking about buying another motor home and driving the Alaskan highway—he never wants to quit! I remember one Easter vacation we took a camping trip to Williamsburg, Virginia. One morning we woke up and my mother commented on how quiet it was. When we opened the tent flaps we discovered it had snowed overnight and our tent was buried in ice and snow. We hurriedly cleaned off the snow, folded up the tent and I remember Dad being worried that the tent material might crack. We ended up staying at a bed and breakfast. Boy, was that nice! On some trips we camped at higher altitudes and I remember being freezing, freezing cold at night. We'd wear all our clothes to bed and there'd be a plastic tablecloth beneath us and one on top of us. Somehow it worked.

His six years at Melody Top Theatre were probably the most exciting for me because there was Dad onstage appearing with these big name stars. The theatre itself was in a huge round tent and I just wish I'd kept an autograph book. Dad would always put us in an aisle seat and when he went past, he'd tip his hat or wave and I'd think, "Oh, that's my dad!" I loved musicals and I memorized all the songs just because I was there so often. My favorite role was when he played Buffalo Bill in *Annie Get Your Gun*. He was dressed all in white—his hat and a beard—and he looked like Colonel Sanders!

My dad was in almost every Melody Top production and I remember one night, in particular, when I got to go all by myself with my dad. I felt very important when he took me backstage to meet the cast and then I got to sit in the audience by myself. Afterwards, we drove home in his little Renault in a terrible rainstorm. The windshield wipers were broken and I had my arm out the window, moving the wipers so we could see.

When I was in Junior High I saw dancers like John Kriza or Tommy Tune perform and, at the time, I didn't realize how important they were. When Dad was appearing with Lee Radziwill in *The Phildelphia Story*, Rudolf Nureyev came to see the show. How I wish I had known so I could have laid eyes on him!

When I was a young child, my dream was to become a ballet dancer. In the 1950's Mom took me to see Balanchine's New York City Ballet do *The Nutcracker* with Maria Tallchief as the Sugar Plum Fairy, Melissa Hayden, and others who are now some of the most famous names in the history of ballet. As I watched, I said to myself, "This is what I want to do!" I remember crying on the train on the way home because I was thinking "How am I going to do this ... how am I going to get there?" But I think my parents didn't realize how deeply I wanted that. They felt I was taking lessons from the best teacher—a family friend who had danced with the Ballet Russe. I think they didn't really want me to pursue that as a profession because it probably would have meant my leaving home for further training. For the past fifteen years I've been teaching ballet in Pensacola, Florida, and I know that if my students want to make it professionally in the dance world, they have to move on to New York or other schools. It's just so competitive now.

I am my father's biggest fan and, to this day, whenever

he walks out onstage, my heart begins to pound. I have such a feeling of pride knowing that's my dad!

Don Thompson, *Bob's Son*

My father's life illustrates the word, "dichotomy". I grew up with a man who revered building a campfire or making sure we all helped put up the tent, but I also saw him receive three standing ovations at a downtown Chicago theatre! I was raised by someone who was regionally famous but was always accessible as a father. Not only accessible but tremendously supportive and tolerant. I always say my dad is the most conservative liberal I know—again the dichotomy. My parents' idea of responsible childrearing was to create avenues of exposures for us in a myriad of ways whether it be theatre, art, music, camping, travel, nature, sports, or dance. My mother would say, "Oh well, we've always felt that about the time you kids reach 18, it's up to you to decide what you want to do."

Somehow my father constructed a genius professional life while being a tremendous family man. As a teenager, I attended many of his rehearsals and I probably saw the show *Status Quo Vadis* thirty-two times from backstage. In *Angel Street* my father played a Sherlock Holmes type detective in tweeds and when you're watching a play and you forget that the character—in this case, Sergeant Rough—is your father, it's obvious that some transcendent art has taken place! My father is an actor's actor; that's a remark which comes from professional circles, be it the guys backstage at the Ivanhoe Theatre, articles about him in the *Chicago Tribune*, or even Earl Wrightson in lead roles at the Melody Top. They've all come to me and said, "Your father is what we call an actor's actor because he's always there for us, we can rely on Bob Thompson."

When I was about 18 years old, I met Truman Capote at the Ivanhoe Theatre when Dad was appearing in *Philadelphia Story*. I had just read *In Cold Blood* and we sat there talking in the back of the theatre for about an hour and a half.

Theatre is magic. I remember I'd go to the Melody Top and watch my father play Buffalo Bill with Jaye P. Morgan in *Annie Get Your Gun* with his singing "There's no business like show business, there's no business I know!" I was right there in the moment, it's my dad onstage and I've got goose-bumps on my arms!

If my father were to be asked "How do you assume a character in a play?" or "What is the source of your inspiration?"—I think he might have some difficulty giving a direct answer. In addition to sound theatrical training and hard work, I believe the ability to act is a gift. In my father's case it is completely intuitive and has often been blessed with a touch of genius!

Index: List of Plays

North Central College

1935   *Much Ado About Nothing*, Wm. Shakespeare

Duluth Summer School of Theatre

1935   *Accent on Youth*, Samson Raphaelson

Goodman Theatre School

1936   *A Winter's Tale*, Wm. Shakespeare
The Prince and the Pauper, Children's Theatre

1937   *Rumpelstiltskin*, Charlotte Chorpenning
Why Marry, Why Not, Jesse Lynch Williams

1938   *Laburnum Grove*, J.B. Priestley
He Who Gets Slapped, Leonid Andreiev
The Adding Machine, Eugene O'Neill
The Circle, Somerset Maugham

1939   *Merry Wives of Windsor*, Wm. Shakespeare
Our Town, Thornton Wilder
Anna Christie, Eugene O'Neill
Bees on the Boat Deck, J.B. Priestley
Goodbye Again, Allan Scott and George Haight
First Lady, Kaufman and Hart

1940   *King Lear*, Wm. Shakespeare

Peninsula Players

1938   *At Mrs. Beam's*, C.K. Munro
Lysistrata, Impromptu, Aristophanes and R.W. Fisher
Night Must Fall, Emlyn Williams

This Mercy We Have Shown, R.W. Fisher
Lady Windermere's Fan, Oscar Wilde
Perish The Thought, Musical Revue
The Dark Tower, Earl Wynn

1939   *The Circle*, Somerset Maugham
Dracula, Bram Stoker
Rain, Somerset Maugham
Dr. Knock, Jules Romaine
The Return of the Barbarians, R.W. Fisher
Salome, Oscar Wilde
Violence Isn't Nice, R.W. Fisher

Plymouth Playhouse, *Milford, Conn.*

1940   *Margin For Error*, Clare Boothe
Our Town, Thornton Wilder
Kiss The Boys Goodbye, Clare Boothe
The Cat and the Canary, John Willard

Hilltop Playhouse, *Ellicott City, Maryland*

1941   *Love From a Stranger*, Frank Vosper
Divorcons, Margaret Mayo
The Gorilla, Ralph Spence
Private Lives, Noel Coward
It's All Done With Memos, Greene and Dibble
No Time for Comedy, S.N. Behrman

1943   *The Battle of Bradley*, New York Stagedoor Canteen

University of Michigan, *Ann Arbor*

1946   *Pigeons and People*, George M. Cohan

1947   *On Borrowed Time*, Paul Osborn

1948   *Candida*, George Bernard Shaw

1949   *The Late George Apley*, John Marquand

Peninsula Players *1953-72*

1953　*The Late Christopher Bean*, Sidney Howard
Harvey, Mary Chase
Boy Meets Girl, Sam and Bella Spewack
Affairs of State, Louis Verneuil
Dover Road, A.A. Milne
Midsummer Madness, R.W. Fisher

1954　*On Borrowed Time*, Paul Osborn
Late Love, Rosemary Casey
Mr. Roberts, Heggen and Logan
Lady's Not For Burning, Christopher Fry
Room Service

1955　*Time Out for Ginger*
Mr. Pim Passes By, A.A. Milne
The Caine Mutiny, Herman Wouk
Sabrina Fair, Samuel Taylor
The Rainmaker, N. Richard Nash

1956　*Dear Charles*
Our Town, Thornton Wilder
Reclining Figure, Harry Kurnitz
Light Up the Sky, Moss Hart
Solid Gold Cadillac, George Kaufman

1957　*Bus Stop*, William Inge
Inherit the Wind, Lawrence and Lee
The Loud Red Patrick, John Boruff
Teahouse of the August Moon, John Patrick
No Time for Sergeants

1964　*A Man For All Seasons*, Robert Bolt

1968　*A Case of Libel*, Henry Denker

1972　*The Tavern*, George M. Cohan
The Skin of Our Teeth, Thornton Wilder
What the Butler Saw, James Orton
Charley's Aunt, Brandon Thomas

Rosary College Theatre *1947–1974*

Death Takes a Holiday

Night Must Fall

Important of Being Earnest

Moor Born

Trojan Women

Electra

The Crucible

A Delicate Balance

Diary of Anne Frank

Song of the Scaffold

Our Town

Time Out for Ginger

The Late Christopher Bean

The Late George Apley

Mad Women of Chaillot

Dear Brutus

Sabrina Fair

Sweethearts

Light Up The Sky

The Righteous Are Bold

The Lady's Not For Burning

The Chester Mystery Cycle

Salt Creek Theatre, *Hinsdale*

1957   *Bus Stop*, William Inge, with Sidney Blackmer and
Barbara Baxley
Jenny Kissed Me, Jean Kerr, with Charlie Ruggles

1958   *Inherit the Wind*, Lawrence and Lee

1959   *The Royal Family*, Kaufman and Ferber, with Linda
Darnell

Tenthouse Music Theatre, *Highland Park*

1958   *Brigadoon*, Lerner and Loewe
The Boyfriend, Sandy Wilson

1959   *Harvey*, Mary Chase, with Joe E. Brown

1964   *Bells Are Ringing*, Comden and Green, with
Robert Q. Lewis

Drury Lane Theatre, *Evergreen Park*

1958   *Affairs of State*, Louis Verneuil, with Constance Moore

1960   *Roman Candle*, Sidney Sheldon, with Tom Duggan

Melody Top Theatre

1960   *Brigadoon*, Lerner and Loewe, with Dennis Day
            Silk Stockings, Cole Porter, with Genevieve
            Annie Get Your Gun, Irving Berlin, with Jaye P. Morgan
            Oklahoma, Rodgers and Hammerstein, with John Raitt
            Kismet

1961   *Bells Are Ringing*, Comden & Green, with Gordon &
            Sheila MacRae
            South Pacific, Rodgers & Hammerstein, with Howard
            Keel
            Take Me Along, with William Bendix
            Anything Goes
            Student Prince
            The King and I, Rogers & Hammerstein, with Jane
            Morgan

1962   *Carousel*, Rodgers & Hammerstein, with Howard Keel
            Kiss Me Kate, with Jane Morgan & Earl Wrightson
            Hit the Deck, Field & Youmans, with Phil Ford & Mimi
            Hines

1963   *The Vagabond King*, Hooker & Post, with Earl
            Wrightson & Lois Hunt
            The Golden Fleecing, Lorenzo Semple, with Bob
            Newhart
            The Music Man, Meredith Wilson, with Forrest Tucker

1964   *The Pajama Game*, Abbott & Brissel, with Phil Ford &
            Mimi Hines

1965   *Camelot*, Lerner & Loewe, with Earl Wrightson & Lois
            Hunt
            South Pacific, Rodgers & Hammerstein, with Betty
            White & Giorgio Tozzi
            Annie Get Your Gun, Irving Berlin, with Jaye P. Morgan

1967   *Carousel*, Rodgers & Hammerstein, with John Raitt

Pheasant Run Theatre, *St. Charles*

1965   *Mr. Roberts*, Heggen & Logan, with Robert Wagner

1967   *George Washington Slept Here*, Hart & Kaufman, with
          June Havoc

1968   *Sabrina Fair*, Samuel Taylor, with Stefanie Powers

Mill Run Playhouse, *Niles*

1968   *Sabrina Fair*, Samuel Taylor, with Kathy Crosby
          Born Yesterday, Garson Kanin, with Betty Grable
          Mister Roberts, Heggen & Logan, with John Gavin

Ivanhoe Theatre

1967   *Philadelphia Story*, Phillip Barry, with Lee Bouvier

1968   *Harvey*, Mary Chase, with Tom Ewell

1969   *Little Foxes*, Lillian Hellman, with Eileen Herlie

1970   *Bus Stop*, William Inge, with Sandy Dennis
          Biggest Thief in Town, Dalton Trombo, with John
          McGiver

1971   *Another Part of the Forest*, Lillian Hellman, with John
          Saxon

1972   *Status Quo Vadis*, Donald Driver, with Gail Strickland
          & David Wilson

1974   *Da*, Hugh Leonard, with John McGiver

Cherry County Playhouse, *Traverse City, Michigan*

1968   *The Rainmaker*

1972   *Affairs of State*, Louis Verneuil- with June Lockhart

Arlington Park Theatre

1972   *Charley's Aunt*, Brandon Thomas, with Louis Nye
         Angel Street, Patrick Hamilton, with Joseph Campanella
         & Margaret Phillips

Playhouse Theatre, *Wilmington, Delaware*

February, 1973
         Status Quo Vadis

Off Broadway Theatre, *San Diego*

December 1973
         Status Quo Vadis, with Ray Walston

Brooks Atkinson Theatre, *New York City*

1973   *Status Quo Vadis*, Donald Driver, with Bruce Boxleitner
         & Ted Danson

Playhouse On The Mall, *Paramus, New Jersey*

May, 1975
         Angel Street, Patrick Hamilton - with Dina Merrill &
         Michael Allinson

Studebaker Theatre, *Chicago*

November, 1975
         Angel Street, Patrick Hamilton, with Dina Merrill &
         Michael Allinson

Peachtree Theatre, *Atlanta, Georgia*

December, 1975
         Angel Street, Patrick Hamilton, with Dina Merrill &
         Michael Allinson

Lyceum Theatre, *New York City*

1975   *Angel Street*, Patrick Hamilton, with Dina Merrill &
         Michael Allinson

Arie Crown Theatre, *McCormick Place*

1974 *Damn Yankees*, Adler, Ross, Abbott, with Gwen Verdon
& Ray Walston
Showboat, Kern & Hammerstein, with Kathryn Grayson
& Mickey Rooney
Oklahoma, Rodgers & Hammerstein, with John
Davidson

Alley Theatre, *Houston, Texas*

1976-77 *The Corn is Green*, Emlyn Williams
You Never Can Tell, George Bernard Shaw
The Runner Stumbles, Milan Stitt

Goodman Theatre

1977 *The Seagull*, Anton Chekhov, with Ruth Ford
Night of the Iguana, Tennessee Williams, with Ruth
Roman, Barbara Rush, Alan Mixon

1978 *Much Ado About Nothing*, Wm. Shakespeare

1979-84 *A Christmas Carol*, Charles Dickens

Candlelight Forum Theatre, *Summit*

1974 *The Real Inspector Hound*, Tom Stoppard
Black Comedy, Peter Shaffer
Solitaire, Double Solitaire, Robert Anderson

1975 *The Good Doctor*, Neil Simon
The Three Cuckolds, Leon Katz
Raisin in the Sun, Lorraine Hansberry
The Gangs All Here, Lawrence & Lee

1976 *God's Favorite*, Neil Simon

1978 *Hello Dolly*, Stewart & Herman
Mame, Lawrence & Lee

1979 *Man From La Mancha*, Wasserman & Lee

1983   *Camelot*, Lerner & Loewe

1993   *It Runs in the Family*, Ray Cooney
          Out of Order, Ray Cooney

1994   *You Can't Take It With You*, Kaufman & Hart

1995   *Carousel*, Rodgers & Hammerstein
          It's a Wonderful Life, Frank Capra

1996   *Funny Money*, Ray Cooney
          Crazy For You, George Gershwin

Northlight Repertory Theatre, *Evanston*

1980   *Angel Street*, Patrick Hamilton, with Greg Vinkler

1981   *On Golden Pond*, Ernest Thompson, with Jean Sincere

World Playhouse, *Chicago*

1981   *On Golden Pond*, Ernest Thompson, with Janet Gaynor

Peninsula Players, *1976 to 2003*

1976   *God's Favorite*, Neil Simon

1977   *California Suite*, Neil Simon
          Equus, Peter Shaffer

1978   *Dracula*, Bram Stoker
          Sly Fox, Molière

1979   *Chapter Two*, Neil Simon
          Da, Hugh Leonard

1980   *Angel Street*, Patrick Hamilton
          On Golden Pond, Ernest Thompson

1981   *Mornings at Seven*, Paul Osborn

1982   *A Life*, Hugh Leonard

1983   *The Middle Ages*, A.R. Gurney
          A Little Family Business, J. Presson Allen
          Foxfire, Susan Cooper & Hume Cronyn

1984   *Painting Churches*, Tina Howe
          Harvey, Mary Chase

1985   *Importance of Being Earnest*, Oscar Wilde
          Noises Off, Michael Frayn

1986   *In the Sweet Bye and Bye*, Donald Driver
          June and the Paycock, Sean Casey
          The Mouse Trap, Agatha Christie

1987   *The Elder Statesman*, T.S. Eliot

1988   *Ten Nights in a Barroom*, Agatha Christie

1989   *The Cocktail Hour*, A.R. Gurney

1990   *The Circle*, Somerset Maugham

1991   *Lend Me a Tenor*, Ken Ludwig
          Other People's Money, Jerry Sterner
          Best Little Whorehouse in Texas, Karen Hall

1992   *Love Letters*, A.R. Gurney

1993   *Dancing at Lughnasa*, Brian Friel
          Out of Order, Ray Cooney

1994   *Pygmalion*, George Bernard Shaw

1995   *You Can't Take it With You*, Kaufman & Hart
          A Funny Thing Happened on the Way to the Forum, Larry
          Gelbart & Stephen Sondheim

1996   *Funny Money*, Ray Cooney
          Crazy For You, George Gershwin

1997   *Guys and Dolls*, Damon Runyon
          Amadeus, Peter Schaffer